HANUMĀN

HANUMĀN

In the Rāmāyaṇa of Vālmīki
and
the Rāmacaritamānasa of Tulasī Dāsa

Catherine Ludvik

MOTILAL BANARSIDASS PUBLISHERS
PRIVATE LIMITED • DELHI

First Edition: Delhi 1994

ISBN: 81-208-1122-4 (Cloth)
ISBN: 81-208-1227-6 (Paper)

Also available at:

MOTILAL BANARSIDASS
41 U.A. Bungalow Road, Jawahar Nagar, Delhi 110007
120 Royapettah High Road, Mylapore, Madras 600 004
16 St. Mark's Road, Bangalore 560 001
Ashok Rajpath, Patna 800 004
Chowk, Varanasi 221 001

PRINTED IN INDIA

BY JAINENDRA PRAKASH JAIN AT SHRI JAINENDRA PRESS,
A-45 NARAINA INDUSTRIAL AREA, PHASE-1, NEW DELHI 110 028
AND PUBLISHED BY NARENDRA PRAKASH JAIN FOR MOTILAL
BANARSIDASS PUBLISHERS PVT. LTD., BUNGALOW ROAD,
JAWAHAR NAGAR, DELHI 110 007

dehabuddhyā tu dāso 'smi
jīvabuddhyā tvad aṃśakaḥ /
ātmabuddhyā tvam evāham
iti me niścitā matiḥ //

From the point of view of the body, I am your servant;
From the point of view of the individual soul, I am a part of you;
From the point of view of the Self, I am you.
This is my conviction.

-attributed to the *Mahānāṭaka*

CONTENTS

PREFACE

The opportunity to spend so much of my time in the last years with Hanumān has been a wonderful experience, a precious gift, and a blessing. My work has been a labour of love, even in the most tedious and minutely technical of moments. Though I was originally drawn to the Hanumān of Tulasī Dāsa's *Rāmacaritamānasa,* a love of the Sanskrit language and an interest in the *Vālmīki Rāmāyaṇa* led me to a comparative study of the two texts. I began to discover Āñjaneya's fascinating multi-faceted character, who, despite his popularity, is the subject of less than a handful of studies. Clearly, my intention was not to remedy completely this neglect, for it would take more than a lifetime to cover adequately such an enormous and seemingly boundless subject, but simply to offer whatever I could within a limited scope. In this, I was aided by Professor Stella Sandahl, my academic supervisor at the University of Toronto, where my work was originally submitted. She always generously gave of her time and attention, she taught me how to read the *Rāmacaritamānasa* in the original Avadhi, and her linguistic ability in both Sanskrit and Hindi was a great asset to me. I was also helped by Swami Tejomayananda, whose lectures on the *Rāmacaritamānasa* and whose chanting of the text I was fortunate enough to attend, and who himself was always ready to answer my questions. His perceptive comments, and perhaps more importantly, his expression and communication of the spirit of Tulasī's work deeply moved me. Furthermore, I owe a very profound debt of gratitude to Swami Chinmayananda, who is responsible for awakening in me the love of things spiritual and things Indian, and whose inspiration and teaching are ever with me. Last but certainly not least, I have been blessed with a wonderful mother and friend, who has been an endless source of support, a dedicated typist, and a meticulous reader of every word I wrote.

Catherine Ludvik

ABBREVIATIONS

Sanskrit Texts

AdhyR	Adhyātma Rāmāyaṇa
Mbh	Mahābhārata
RV	Ṛg Veda
ValR	Vālmīki Rāmāyaṇa
crit. ed.	Critical edition of the *Vālmīki Rāmāyaṇa* prepared by the Baroda Oriental Institute
KKlf	R.J. Lefeber's annotated translation of the Kiṣkindhākāṇḍa

Classical Hindi Texts (Works of Tulaṣī Dāsa)

D	Dohāvalī
G	Gītāvalī
HB	Hanumān Bāhuka
K	Kavitāvalī
RCM	Rāmacaritamānasa
VP	Vinaya Patrikā

Journals

ABORI	Annals of the Bhandarkar Oriental Research Institute
IA	Indian Antiquary
JAOS	Journal of the American Oriental Society
JOIB	Journal of the Oriental Institute, Baroda
JRAS	Journal of the Royal Asiatic Society
OLP	Orientalia Lovaniensia Periodica

NOTE ON EDITIONS AND TRANSLITERATION

I have used the critical edition of the *Vālmīki Rāmāyaṇa*, prepared by the Baroda Oriental Institute, and the Geeta Press edition of the *Rāmacaritamānasa* throughout. For the other works of Tulasī Dāsa, the numbering of the verses refers to the *Tulasī Granthāvalī* (Varanasi: Nāgarīpracāriṇī Sabhā, 1973).

I have adopted the standard transliteration for Sanskrit words and quotations. This was also applied to passages in Classical Hindi, since the inherent "a" (as in Rām*a*) is metrically significant.

Catherine Ludvik

1

INTRODUCTION

Hanumān, Māruti, Pavanakumāra, Vāyusuta, Āñjaneya, Kesarinandana, Mahāvīra, Bajaraṅgī, Saṅkaṭamocana... a small monkey figure kneeling with joined palms beside Rāma, Lakṣmaṇa, and Sītā, sometimes tearing his chest open to show Rāma's image in his heart, other times flying through the sky with a Himalayan peak in his hand, long-haired, occasionally five-headed, hands in fear-removing (*abhaya*) and wish-granting (*varada*) *mudrās,*[1] carrying club, bow, and thunderbolt... devoted and providing devotion, compassionate yet fierce, protector and remover of obstacles, giver of prosperity and destroyer of evil[2] . . . all these are Hanumān. Multi-faceted, it is impossible to embrace every one of his manifestations in one sweep. Some of his characteristics are very ancient, others, relatively recent, and still others are appearing even now. In an attempt to understand some of these, a comparison of Hanumān as he is presented in the *Rāmāyaṇa* of Vālmīki and the *Rāmacaritamānasa* of Tulasī Dāsa is undertaken herein.[3] Since it would prove misleading to isolate completely this study from prior, posterior, as well as intervening developments in his characterization, general information precedes and also follows the comparative analysis.

As Hanumān is said to be a monkey, the identity and the symbolism of monkeys are examined. Then, the focus is narrowed down to Hanumān: his origins and his associations. A study of the development of his character within the ValR, between the ValR and the RCM, as well as Tulasī Dāsa's own perception of Hanumān follows. Once the preliminaries have been covered, a scene-by-scene comparative analysis of the two chosen texts is taken up, after which, a brief outline of the growth of Hanumān's figure from Tulasī Dāsa's time onwards leads up to the present.

It is important to understand here that development may be interpreted at different levels: from a historical point of view, the portraits painted in the two texts represent stages in the evolution of a Hanumān cult; from a symbolical point of view, the texts gradually open up more, and perhaps deeper, levels of the Hanumān symbol; from a theological point of view, Hanumān unfolds from an ideal messenger to one with supernatural powers and eventually to a deity in his own right.[4] Therefore, as we enter upon this bird's-eye view of his development, all three of these levels should simultaneously be kept in mind so as not to take too narrow a perspective and incur loss in the process.

The Monkeys

There has been much discussion concerning the identity of those who come under the headings of *vānara, hari, kapi, plavaga, plavaṃgama, śākhāmṛga, golāṅgūla*—all descriptive epithets[5] which over time came to mean "monkey"— as well as *ṛkṣa* (yet another species of monkey).[6] Are they monkeys (*vānaras*) or men (*vā naras*)? Many scholars have argued in favour of tribals with, perhaps, a monkey banner.[7] G. Ramadas infers from Rāvaṇa's reference to the *kapis'* tail as an ornament (*bhūṣaṇa*)[8] that it is a long appendage in the dress worn by men of the Savara tribe. Since the women did not wear this "long piece of cloth", he continues, Vālmīki does not describe them as monkeys.[9] In the Sanskrit epic, on the one hand they are presented very much as humans with reference to their speech, clothing (4:10:21), habitations (4:32:9-13), funerals (4:24:24), consecrations (4:25:20) etc., and on the other, as monkeys with reference to their leaping (4:2:9-11) and their hair (4:66:1) and fur (4:17:33).[10] In conflict situations, their conduct may appear rather beastly, as in the Vālin-Sugrīva relationship, and yet in some ways it is more human than that of their idealized "human" counterparts.[11]

F. Whaling adds the third possibility of semi-divine beings, based on their supernatural strength and actions.[12] Likewise, the *Tilaka*, a commentary on the ValR, points out that the ability of the *vānaras* to take any form at will (*kāmarūpin*) conforms to the nature of gods.[13] In fact, in the ValR (1:16:6-7),[14] as well as in the *Adhyātma Rāmāyaṇa*[15] (1:2:30; 7:3) and the RCM (1:do.187), Brahmā commands the gods either to bear monkey offspring[16] or directly to incarnate as monkeys in order to assist Rāma in his mission.

Since the Rāma story (*Rāmakathā*) is not history, but rather legend, it may prove more fruitful to examine what the *vānaras* symbolize.[17] Generally, they represent unchastity,[18] and more broadly speaking, the instinctual personality and the baser human propensities,[19] such as carnal instincts, duplicity, trickery, cunning etc. Due to the monkeys' fickleness (*nityam asthiracitta*)[20] and inability to remain still (*anavasthita*)[21] even for a moment—characteristics, as Hanumān himself admits (ValR 5:53:11), for which they are known throughout the three worlds—they symbolize the agitated mind. The very word *kapi* comes from *kamp*, meaning "to tremble" or "to shake", and thus to be unsteady. *Śākhāṃrgatva* is defined, yet again by Āñjaneya, as lightness of mind (*laghucittatā*)[22] and lack of concentration (*ātmānaṃ na sthāpayasi yo matau*).[23] Therefore, when all thoughts (monkeys) are brought under the control of the Lord[24] (Rāma), through their combined force, ignorance crystallized into the form of the ego (Rāvaṇa) is defeated. As for Hanumān, his special position of successful leadership embodies the quality of self-control (*brahmacarya* in the broadest sense), for which he later becomes known.[25]

Hanumān's Origins and Associations

Regarding Hanumān's origin, there is general consensus about his *yakṣa*, and therefore non-Aryan, provenance. As R.N. Misra explains, *yakṣas* were originally conceptually fluid, but "eventually assumed a corporeality invested with character and attributes, and through a historical process of transformation, altered so much that what had . . . started as a nebulous idea, somewhat enigmatic in context, ultimately assumed demonic [or beneficient] attributes and functions."[26] They came to be worshipped in the form of mounds of earth—one of the ways in which Hanumān is venerated even today.[27] Though *yakṣas* could assume any form at will, they became animal-headed cult deities,[28] a number of them dwelling in trees.[29] As vegetation spirits, they bestowed abundance in the widest sense of the term so as to include fertility on the one hand, and material wealth on the other (thus the association with Kubera).[30] They have been and are still revered as tutelary deities of villages, doorkeepers (*dvārapālas*) of temples, givers of offspring, protectors against disease—the same chief aspects of the Hanumān cult.[31] Furthermore, *yakṣas* are *vīras*,[32] or as they are known and worshipped today, *bīra-barahms*,[33] and Hanumān is repeatedly and increasingly referred to as *vīra*,[34] *pravīra*,[35] and eventually the dominant *mahāvīra*,[36] the popular deity of the Hindi-speaking areas.[37] While the *Skanda* (1:2:27-29) and *Matsya* (154:542-78) *Purāṇas* identify a certain Vīraka, a son of Śiva, as the latter's gatekeeper, the Bengali *Kṛttivāsa Rāmāyaṇa*[38] allots that function to Hanumān. Furthermore, in Uttar Pradesh, Mahāvīra's birthday is celebrated on Dīpāvalī night—the very same night which in ancient times, according to the *Kāmasūtra* (1:4:27), was known as *yakṣarātri*, the biggest *yakṣa* festival of the year.[39] However, A.K. Coomaraswamy has argued on the basis of the *Skanda Purāṇa's* list of Hanumān's twelve names, which do not refer to his classical *yakṣa* functions, but focus rather on his characterization as presented in the ValR, that his veneration arose independently from his *yakṣa* association.[40] It would then appear that *yakṣa*-Hanumān's popularity was spurred by his incorporation into the *Rāmakathā*, whence, over time, both of these aspects (especially the first)[41] gained prominence.

F.E. Pargiter[42] has identified the *Ṛg Veda's*[43] Vṛṣākapi with Hanumān. Noting the close connection of a portion of the *Brahma Purāṇa* (77-175) with RV 10:86, he has argued his case on a textual basis. The Purāṇic account (129:11-125) tells of Indra's defeat at the hands of Mahāśani and his consequent attempt at rehabilitating himself through the worship of Śiva and Viṣṇu. Abjaka Vṛṣākapi, who has the appearance of both Śiva and Viṣṇu, is born and kills Mahāśani, thereby becoming a friend of Indra. The RV hymn begins here with Vṛṣākapi's monopolization of offerings intended for Indra.[44] When the latter's favourite defiles Indrāṇī's "precious, well-made, anointed things",[45] she is furious,[46] but to no avail, for her husband merely tries to console her so as to reconcile her with Vṛṣākapi.

A second story found in the *Brahma Purāṇa* (84:1-20) establishes, according to Pargiter, a connection between the names "Hanumān" and "Vṛṣākapi": the Godāvarī-Phenā confluence, where Hanumān helped Kesarin's second wife Adrikā to liberate herself from a curse by bathing there, "obtained in consequence not only the names Mārjāra and Hanūmat . . . but also that of Vṛṣākapi . . ."[47] The problem is, however, that these appellations are not synonymous of one and the same place, but rather are different sacred places (*tīrthas*) alongside one another at the Phenāsaṃgama: the text specifies that "beyond" (*tasmāt*) Mārjāra are Hanūmat and Vṛṣākapi (84:19).[48] Furthermore, the differentiation between these *tīrthas* is confirmed in a later passage (129:1-2) where the Indratīrtha, Vṛṣākapa(tīrtha), Hanūmat(tīrtha), and Abjaka(tīrtha) are not adjectival to one another, but a cumulative (*ca*) list.[49]

Pargiter also states that *vṛṣā-kapi*, "male monkey", is the Sanskrit translation of the Dravidian *āṇ-mandi*,[50] which has also been Sanskritized into "Hanumant".[51] K.C. Chattopadhyaya and U.P. Shah both reject the Dravidian origin of *vṛṣākapi*, as well as the identification with Hanumān or any other monkey.[52] Shah's argument, on the linguistic level, is based on the necessity of an additional step between "Hanumant" and "Hanumān".[53] He further points out that no explicit identification or association of Vṛṣākapi with Hanumān is to be found anywhere in Vedic or later Indian literature. On the contrary, Viṣṇu (*Viṣṇusahasranāma Stotra*,[54] verse 47), as well as one of the Rudras (*Mahābhārata*[55] 13:150:12ff.) are given the appellation "Vṛṣa".[56] The *Brahma Purāṇa* (124:100-102) itself calls Śiva "Vṛṣākapi". Furthermore, the Mbh (12:330:24) gives the meaning of Vṛṣākapi as "*dharma* in the form of the best *varāha*", which, in Shah's view, is a rhinoceros,[57] and in Chattopadhyaya's view, the sun poetically described.[58] According to Sanskrit lexicographers, *kapis* can indeed be animals other than monkeys.[59] Moreover, the *Brahma Purāṇa* version of the myth clearly states that Vṛṣākapi is a "man" (*puruṣa*) born of water (129:98). It may also be noted that while the latter, according to Sāyaṇa,[60] is the son of Indra, Hanumān is that of Vāyu; and whereas Vṛṣākapi has a wife (RV 10:86:13), Āñjaneya, as he appears in India,[61] is unmarried.[62] Therefore, it is impossible to accept any connection between *yakṣa*-Hanumān and Vṛṣākapi.

Apart from the above posed identification, many comparisons of Hanumān to various characters, both within the Hindu fold and outside of it, have been suggested. Since Jacobi, for instance, understood the abduction and recovery of Sītā to be an agricultural myth paralleled on the RV's Indra-Vṛtra episode (1:32:1-15), he argued in favour of a connection between Hanumān and Indra, the bringers of the monsoon, both of whose appellations have the same meaning: while Hanumān is one with (*mat*) a jaw (*hanu*), Indra's *śipravat* attribute (RV 6:17:2), according to the *Nirukta* (6:17), signifies "possessing a jaw bone" (*śipre hanū nāsike vā*).[63] Jacobi also compared Hanumān to Indra's dog Saramā who finds the stolen cows (RV 10:108), just as Hanumān finds Sītā.[64]

As for comparisons to characters outside of the Hindu world, Odysseus, Joshua,[65] and Gilgamesh[66] may be noted. In fact, it is possible to compare Hanumān to any hero on the standard mythological adventure quest,[67] for the pattern of separation from the known realm, encounter of fabulous forces, ultimate victory, and return corresponds at every step.

The Development of Hanumān's Character from the ValR to the RCM

In our discussion of the evolution of Hanumān's character, it is helpful to resort to the four stages enumerated by C. Bulcke:[68]

A. Original Rāma-ballads
B. Authentic ValR

C. Vulgate ValR

D. Medieval *Rāmāyaṇa* Literature.

In the initial stage, itinerant storytellers orally recited not only ballads, but also small songs and even stray verses.[69] This age would correspond to a period prior to the third century B.C.E.[70]— very likely a number of centuries prior to it. As Bulcke explains, Hanumān had not yet come to be associated with Añjanā and would remain so until the third stage. He was known to the bards as "Vāyuputra" (an appellation which did not come into vogue until the second stage) long before they knew him as "Añjanīputra" or "Kesarinandana", as is clear from the extreme rarity of references to both Añjanā and Kesarin in the vulgate. Evidently, the accounts of Hanumān's birth were later interpolations.[71] Thus far, his most stressed qualities were courage and shrewdness.

In the following stage, the Authentic ValR, after many generations of balladists had sung the *Rāmakathā*, expanding, embellishing, and abridging it according to their own tastes and the responses of their audiences,[72] Vālmīki in about the third century B.C.E. composed, on the basis of these creative re-tellings, the *Rāmāyaṇa*. Roughly, this would correspond to Books Two through Six in a shorter and more simplified form.[73] Herein, as Hanumān's feats were being gradually magnified, the epithet "Vāyuputra" was assigned to him, for at the time, according to H. Lüders,[74] the word was understood to mean conjurer (*vidyādhara*). Lüders also notes the *Sumagga Jātaka* story of *vidyādhara* Vāyussa Putto.[75] Thus, Hanumān's qualities of shrewdness and courage continued to dominate, but his stature steadily increased.

Then, in about the second century C.E.[76] in the Vulgate ValR stage, Books One and Seven were added. Rāma was now recognized as an incarnation of Viṣṇu, and Vālmīki, as a legendary personage—a thief turned seer (*ṛṣi*)[77]—who had been a contemporary of Rāma.[78] The bards continued to add material, such as Hanumān's birth and youthful adventures, and further amplified the extent of his exploits. He was transformed into the actual son of the Wind (Vāyu) and of a celestial nymph (*apsaras*) named Puñjikasthalā (Mbh

1:114:53) who had been cursed to become a monkey and was known as Āñjanā (ValR 4:65:8-18; 7:35:20). What originally seems to have been a swim across perhaps a shallow patch of the ocean[79] became an astonishing leap (5:1), to which a series of other feats were added, such as the burning of Laṅkā (5:52), flying to the Himalayas, bringing back a mountain peak to the battle site (6:61, 89), and jumping at the sun (4:65:19; 7:35:23). He also became an expert in grammar (7:36:42), which in later times was expanded to scholarship in general, astrology, music, and poetry.[80] According to Bulcke, Hanumān's new found immortality (*cirañjīvatva*) originated in a literal reading of the immortality of his fame: Rāma's bestowal on him of the boon of remaining in the world so long as the *Rāmakathā* is being sung (7:39:16-18) is interpreted by Bulcke as referring, at least in the Mbh (3:275:43) version thereof, to Āñjaneya's fame rather than his life.[81] To be noted also in this connection is the belief that immortal Hanumān lives in the Himalayas, as is illustrated in the Mbh (3:146-47).[82] Thus in the vulgate stage, Hanumān became far more than just shrewd and courageous: he was now *cirañjīva* and Āñjaneya.

It is possible to look at the development of Hanumān's characterization within the ValR in three consecutive steps, which would correspond to Bulcke's Authentic ValR and Vulgate ValR stages:[83]

(a) In the *Kiṣkindhākāṇḍa* he is the ideal, though ordinary, minister (*saciva*).
(b) In the *Sundarakāṇḍa* he acquires a supernatural and ever-expanding dimension in his powers and feats.[84]
(c) In the *Uttarakāṇḍa*, an attempt is made to bring steps (a) and (b) in line with one another by explaining, by means of a curse, why so powerful a monkey could not protect Sugrīva from Vālin (7:35:11-16; 7:36:28-33).

A. Wurm[85] has defined the *Kiṣkindhākāṇḍa* and *Sundarakāṇḍa* steps as the general and the functional conceptions of Hanumān: generally, as the ideal minister, he is a reconnoiteur, a counsellor, and a messenger; but when his character is intended to bring awe, wonderment, and thrill to the audience, he is endowed with superhuman powers and skills, in addition to demolition rage and fighting ardour. Though he is usually humble and discreet, for functional purposes, he becomes boastful, bombastic, and self-assertive. His prudence gives way to pugnacity, his proficiency in speech (*vākyajña*)[86] to proficiency in battle.[87]

Bulcke's final stage in the characterization of Hanumān moves outside of the ValR, concerning itself with the Medieval *Rāmāyaṇa* Literature, of which there is a great deal. Prior to this period, however, the *Rāmopākhyāna* of the Mbh (3:257-75) had already been brought to existence. It had taken shape during the stage of the Vulgate ValR. About 400 C.E., Kālidāsa composed the *Raghuvaṃśa*, and following him, Bhavabhūti in the seventh or eighth century wrote the *Mahāvīracarita* and the *Uttararāmacarita*. The eleventh century[88] *Mahānāṭaka*,[89] a very sizeable play[90] traditionally attributed to Hanumān,[91] half of which consists in compilations[92] from other works,[93] presented an underlying *bhakti* current and was later followed by many *Rāmāyaṇas*. Jayadeva's *Prasanna Rāghava*,[94] a drama, appeared *c.*1200, by which time the *Agastya Saṃhitā*,[95] a basic devotional text for the Rāma cult, had been written. Many of the *Purāṇas* (*c.*300-1500)[96] included *Rāmakathā* accounts of varying lengths,[97] and one even admitted a *Hanumatkathā*.[98] *Rāmāyaṇas* appeared in different languages, such as the Tamil *Kamba Rāmāyaṇa* (c.1200) and the Bengali *Kṛttivāsa Rāmāyaṇa* (1346). There were also a number of sectarian *Rāmāyaṇas*, some of which (*Yoga Vāsiṣṭha* and *Adbhuta*[99]) are traditionally ascribed to Vālmīki: the *Bhuṣuṇḍi*, dating back to about the twelfth century,[100] focuses on the love play of Rāma and Sītā and on esoteric *bhakti*; the *Yoga Vāsiṣṭha*, a popular and very lengthy twelfth to thirteenth century[101] text on Advaita Vedānta, is a didactic dialogue between Rāma and Vasiṣṭha; the fifteenth century[102] *Mūla* and *Ānanda*, which are important to the followers of Madhva, describe the importance of Hanumān; the *Adhyātma* (1490-1550),[103] a revered scripture of the Rāmānandi *sādhus*, which is said to be part of the *Brahmāṇḍa Purāṇa*, attempts to integrate Vedāntic views of Rāma into

Purāṇic and Tāntric views of Him;[104] and the *Adbhuta*,[105] a "comparatively modern" text with both Vaiṣṇava and Śākta elements, gives long accounts of the origins of the incarnation of Rāma and Sītā. Two *Upaniṣads*, the *Rāmatāpanīya*[106] and the *Rāmarahasya*, belong to the sixteenth and the seventeenth centuries[107] and glorify Rāma as the Supreme Person (*parama puruṣa*) and Sītā as the Cause of creation (*mūla prakṛti*). Another seventeenth century text is the *Tattvasaṃgraha Rāmāyaṇa* written by Rāmabrahmānanda "as a definite compendium of all the forms of the Rāma story".[108]

In this brief survey, the ValR commentaries cannot be neglected: *Vivekatilaka* by Uḍāli Varadarāja dating back to 1250, *Rāmānujīya* of the fourteenth to the fifteenth century by Rāmānuja, *Tattvadīpikā* from the middle of the sixteenth century by Maheśvaratīrtha, and *Bhūṣaṇa* of the fifteenth to the seventeenth century by Govindarāja, to name but the most important.[109] All of these—in fact, all Indian commentaries on the ValR—are devotional in their outlook, for they view Rāma as an incarnation of Viṣṇu.

In this stage of the Medieval *Rāmāyaṇa* Literature, Bulcke points to four new characteristics acquired by Hanumān:

a) Incarnation of Śiva
b) Founder of *Rāmabhakti*
c) *Brahmacarya*
d) Veneration.

The first may have its origin in the Śaivaites' desire to share in the *Rāmakathā*'s ever-increasing popularity.[110] Furthermore, and to the advantage of the Śaivaites, the *Vedas* maintain the association of the Maruts with Rudra.[111] They are the sons of Rudra, and Hanumān, as the son of the Wind, therefore finds parentage with and eventually becomes an incarnation (*avatāra*) of Śiva. A link in this process of identification of Vāyusuta with the Vedic Maruts and ultimately with Rudra may be found in the *Agni Purāṇa* (51:16), wherein Hanumān is described as holding a thunderbolt (*vajra*)[112] —the very instrument which the Maruts hold in the RV (1:64:5; 1:168:8). The connection with Śiva is firmly established by the tenth century C.E. and perhaps even as early as the eighth century.[113] The *Bhaviṣya* (2:4:13:31-36), *Brahmavaivarta* (4:47:62-63), *Bṛhaddharma* (18), *Mahābhāgavata* (37), *Śiva* (3:20), and *Skanda* (5:2:79; 5:3:84) *Purāṇas*, as well as the *Mahānāṭaka* (5:33; 6:27), the *Ānanda* (1:11), *Kamba* (5:13), *Kṛttivāsa* (6:129), and *Tattvasaṃgraha* (4:12; 7:2) *Rāmāyaṇas* see Hanumān as *Rudrāvatāra*.[114] Jñāneśvara in his commentary on the *Bhagavad Gītā*, the *Bhāvārthadipikā* (1:141), refers to him as the incarnation of Śaṅkara, seated on Arjuna's flagstaff (as a fulfilment of his promise to Bhīma in Mbh 3:150:15). The *Bhaviṣya* and *Śiva Purāṇas* and the *Tattvasaṃgraha Rāmāyaṇa* give detailed accounts of his birth from Śiva and Añjanā,[115] the latter of whom may be interpreted, in the Govardhana region, as a form of Kālī.[116] In fact, in the *Kamba Rāmāyaṇa*, Hanumān is the son of Śiva and Pārvatī.[117] Furthermore, E.W. Hopkins has noted a resemblance between Hanumān and Skanda already in the ValR,[118] which may also have given a slight impetus to the progressive identification with Śiva. And reaching back to Hanumān's *yakṣa* origins, it may be noted that Coomaraswamy points to a close formal relationship between the oldest known Śiva images (Guḍimallam *liṅga*) and the *yakṣas* of Bhārhut and Sāñcī.[119]

The *Rudrāvatāra* conception is carried forward in Tulasī Dāsa's *Vinaya Patrikā* (26:1; 27:1, 3; 29:5), *Dohāvalī* (127-28), and *Hanumān Bāhuka* (9,14),[120] as well as Nābhā Dāsa's *Bhakta Mālā*,[121] in all of which Śiva incarnates as Hanumān for the express purpose of serving Rāma. One also finds the association in the Oriya Mbh of Śāraḷā Dāsa, Tukarāma's works,[122] Mahipati's *Santavijaya*,[123] and the Siamese *Rāmakien*,[124] to name but a few instances. In Bhojpuri folktales, Hanumān receives *śakti* from Śiva and Pārvatī, and thereby becomes an incarnation thereof, giving it identifiable form and personality.[125] In this light, it is due to Śiva's *śakti* that he is able to express supernatural powers and perform such great feats.

Closely related to Hanumān's association with Śiva is Bulcke's third characteristic, *brahmacarya*,[126] which Hanumān comes to share with Śaṅkara, the great ascetic. The earliest reference to this quality in relation to Āñjaneya is to be found in the *Skanda Purāṇa* (5:3:83).[127] It may be traced, in the ValR, to Hanumān's obsession with propriety: when, during his search through Laṅkā, he has observed *rākṣasīs* asleep, he scrutinizes the correctness of his action, finally concluding that he has not misbehaved due to the purity of his intentions and the unaffected condition of his mind (5:9:34-42). Therefore, though the attribute arises in the ValR, Śiva's possession thereof enhances the impetus to identify Hanumān with the latter.

In Śāralā Dāsa's Oriya Mbh, Arjuna Dāsa's *Rāmavibhā*, and the Marāthi *Bhāvārtha Rāmāyaṇa* (7:35), Hanumān is said to be born with a *vajra* loincloth (*vajrakaupīna*),[128] symbolizing his adamantine establishment in *brahmacarya*. It is, therefore, not surprising that the loinclothed ones (*kaupīnavants*),[129] the renunciates and particularly the Śaivaite ones,[130] regard him highly. The Nāth *yogīs* worship him as a great *yogī* (*mahāyogī*), and he is represented in their forehead mark.[131]

If the meaning of *brahmacarya* is taken in its original and literal sense, it signifies far more than celibacy or even general self-control. One who wanders and by extension lives in *Brahman* (a *brahmacārin*) is also a knower of *Brahman* (a *brahmajñānin*). Tulasī Dāsa extolls Hanumān as the foremost among the *jñānins* (*jñāninām agragaṇyam*).[132]

The second characteristic, that of being the founder of *Rāmabhakti*, acquired by Hanumān during Bulcke's Medieval *Rāmāyaṇa* Literature stage, is intimately related to the unfoldment of the Rāma figure to the position of Supreme God.[133] Hanumān can no longer be merely a messenger or even an ordinary devotee (*bhakta*); he must be, at the very least, the ideal *bhakta*. The *Bhāgavata Purāṇa* (5:19:1) refers to him as the foremost worshipper of the Lord (*parama bhāgavata*), and the *Bhakta Mālā* (7:9), as the nineteenth of the forty-two beloved ones of Viṣṇu (*Harivallabhas*).[134] His privilege of being present wherever and whenever the *Rāmāyaṇa* is being recited (*Ānanda Rāmāyaṇa* 1:12:143;

Tattvasaṃgraha Rāmāyaṇa 5:11; *Kṛttivāsa Rāmāyaṇa*) stems from the boon which, in the ValR (7:39:16), he asks for from Rāma; that is, to remain alive so long as the *Rāmakathā* is being sung. In several texts, such as the *Rāmarahasya Upaniṣad* and the *Hanumat* and *Śiva Saṃhitās*, he becomes a teacher of *Rāmabhakti*, and in the *Śiva Purāṇa* (3:20:36) he is said to have established devotion to Rāma in the world. At this point, he himself becomes an object of veneration (Bulcke's fourth characteristic), for through his ideal example and now through his intervention and blessings, he provides access to Rāma.[135] His identification with Śiva is further reason, and according to Bulcke[136] the reason, for his worship. Already in the *Skanda Purāṇa* (5:3:83:29), there is evidence of the practice of repeating the names of Hanumān, which exercise is said to be beneficial for the world. Between the tenth and the fifteenth century, his worship becomes widespread, assuming its own distinct features. His primary functions, then just as today, are the removal of obstacles and the protection against evil spirits and disease[137]—characteristics of *yakṣa*-Hanumān, who seems to have greatly benefited in popularity from his inclusion in the *Rāmakathā*.

Before we enter upon the study of Tulasī Dāsa's perception of and relationship to Hanumān, a summing-up of what has thus far been covered may prove helpful. Originally a *yakṣa*, Hanumān was incorporated into the ValR, wherein, as his feats were gradually magnified by the balladists, he came to be viewed as Vāyuputra (a *vidyādhara*). Eventually, this appellation began to be taken literally, and his parentage with the Wind was extended to the association of the Vedic Maruts with Rudra. He became *Rudrāvatāra*, and this, coupled with his increasing status of ideal *Rāmabhakta* and eventually founder of *Rāmabhakti*—a development parallel to the unfoldment of the Rāma figure—led to the very popular worship of Hanumān in a similar form to that of his *yakṣa* origins. In brief, he seems to have gone full circle, though in the process acquiring a more elaborate and distinct character, as well as far and wide renown.

For Tulasī Dāsa (1543-1623),[138] who is traditionally said to have been a reincarnation of Vālmīki,[139] Hanumān is particularly important. Apart from seeing him as Rāma's messenger and ideal devotee, Tulasī considers him to be learned in Vedānta (VP 26:8), the best of *Sāma Veda* singers (VP 27:3), a scriptural, Vedic, and grammatic commentator (VP 28:5), a poet, one proficient in many arts (VP 28:5), and the author of the *Mahānāṭaka* (VP 29:3).[140] In his works, he frequently refers to the power of Hanumān's name and urges his readers to dwell on it and repeat it (D 212, 214; HB 14,15,17). Hanumān is the wishfulfilling tree for the Kali age[141] (HB 9) and the remover of all difficulties (HB 17, 20).

According to M.P. Gupta,[142] Tulasī Dāsa became associated with a Hanumān temple at an early age. He is also said to have built one, if not ten, temples in honour of Āñjaneya.[143] As the intermediary between the devotee and Rāma (HB 21), Hanumān is credited for putting Tulasī in Rāma's care (HB 40). Priyā Dāsa[144] relates how, advised by a ghost, Tulasī met Hanumān at a recitation of the *Rāmāyaṇa* and asked him for a vision of Rāma. However, when the Lord appeared before him in a human form, Tulasī did not recognize Him, and according to Mahipati's *Bhaktavijaya* (3:131), petitioned Hanumān for another manifestation of Rāma. This time he did recognize the Lord with bow and arrow.

Tulasī always turned to Hanumān in times of distress, such as in his old age when he was afflicted with pain, on which occasion he wrote the *Hanumān Bāhuka.* Priyā Dāsa narrates how the emperor of Delhi threw Tulasī into jail for the latter's inability to perform a miracle before him. When the prisoner invoked Hanumān, many thousands of monkeys (Hanumān's army) began to destroy the palace, the capital, and the people. Alarmed, the king begged Tulasī's forgiveness and immediately released him.[145] In a further incident, when the Varanasi *paṇḍits,* outraged at Tulasī's use of the vernacular rather than chaste Sanskrit, had a tāntric invoke Bhairava so as to destroy the author, Hanumān rescued him.[146] Other episodes relate how Āñjaneya protected him from robbers[147] and was even instrumental in saving him from Kali *yuga,*[148] who had become angry because Tulasī was saving so many souls. The latter circumstance led to the composition, at

Hanumān's suggestion, of the *Vinaya Patrikā* (*Letter of Petition*), which was then delivered to Rāma by Hanumān himself.[149]

Hanumān became especially popular in Northern India after Tulasī Dāsa had given him such an important place in his works and in his life.[150] Though it is true that the traditional accounts of the author's life are "traditional" rather than "biographical", his own writings[151] clearly reflect his great devotion to Hanumān. The legends that have sprung up around Tulasī are magnified manifestations of his *Hanumadbhakti*, which is by no means "legendary".

REFERENCES

1. Hand gestures or positions.
2. For iconographical representations of Hanumān, see Jouveau-Dubreuil 1937, p. 82; Liebert 1976, p.100; Mallmann 1963, p. 50; H.K. Sastri 1974, pp. 64-65.
3. From here onwards, Vālmīki's *Rāmāyaṇa* and Tulasī Dāsa's *Rāmacaritamānasa* are abbreviated to ValR and RCM, respectively.
4. Adapted from the explanation concerning the development of Rāma's figure in Whaling 1980, p. 319.
5. The forest-dwelling *vānara*, the reddish-brown or yellow *hari*, the trembling *kapi*, the leaping *plavaga* and *plavaṃgama*, the branch gazelle *śākhāmṛga*, and the cow-tailed *golāṅgūla*.
6. See KKlf, vol.1, pp. xx-xxi. More broadly speaking, Goldman (1989) considers them to be primates.
7. Ramadas 1925; A.V. Russel (*Tribes and Castes of the Central Provinces*, vol.1, p. 90) referred to in Bulcke 1959-60, p. 396; Sankalia 1973, p. 49; Thapar 1978, p.14; Vyas 1967, p. 23.
8. ValR 5:51:3.
9. See also Masson 1981, p. 357, note 4.
10. KKlf, vol.1, p. xix.
11. Ibid., p. xxv. The behaviour of one of the idealized human counterparts, Rāma, is discussed on p.35 of the present study.
12. Whaling 1980, p. 27, note 1.
13. Masson 1981, p. 356.
14. Though the *Bālakāṇḍa* is a later portion of the text (see Jacobi 1893, p. 64), this reference is noted because the present study does not deal merely with "the original *Rāmāyaṇa*", but extends to Tulasī Dāsa's reading of it.
15. Henceforth abbreviated to AdhyR.
16. Sugrīva, for instance, is the offspring of the Sun (ValR 3:68:16), and Vālin, that of Indra (ValR 4:11:37).

17. Thapar 1978, p. 3.
18. The *Kathāsaritsāgara* refers to an adulterous *brahman* who is changed into a monkey (KKlf, vol.1, p. lxvi, note 44). Likewise, in the ValR (5:35:31), Sītā, who will not willingly allow herself to be touched by any male other than Rāma, considers Hanumān's offer to carry her across the ocean to be an expression of his monkey nature (*kapitva*).
19. Dunnigan 1987, p. 65.
20. ValR 4:53:9. *Anavasthita* (5:53:11) also conveys the meaning of fickleness.
21. ValR 5:53:11.
22. The *Tilaka* then glosses this term as mental unsteadiness (*capala*), which, like *kapi*, comes from *kamp*. The *Amṛtakataka* commentary also gives this explanation (KKlf, vol. 2, note on 4:2:16).
23. ValR 4:2:16.
24. Or leader in the earliest layer of the ValR.
25. Over time, as Hanumān's character developed, he came to symbolize many different aspects, as for instance, *śakti* on the one hand, and *bhakti* on the other. See pp.11-13.
26. Misra 1979, p. vii.
27. V.S. Agrawal ("Vīra Barahma" in *Janapada* [Varanasi] 1:3, pp. 64-73) referred to in Bulcke 1959-60, p. 402; Agrawal 1970, p.186.
28. Misra 1979, pp.132-35.
29. Coomaraswamy 1928-31, part 2, plates 25:1-4.
30. Ibid., part 1, p. 8; part 2, p.13.
31. Bulcke 1959-60, p.402.
32. Ibid.; Agrawal 1970, pp. 166,172,185.
33. Agrawal 1970, p.166.
34. Thirty-three times in the crit. ed. of the *Kiṣkindhā* and *Sundara kāṇḍas*.
35. Eight times in the crit. ed. of the *Kiṣkindhā* and *Sundara kāṇḍas*.
36. E.g. RCM 1:17:5.
37. Ghurye 1962, p. 229.
38. Sen 1920, p. 47.
39. Agrawal 1970, pp. 186, 86.
40. Coomaraswamy 1928-31 referred to in Bulcke 1959-60, p.402.
41. See p.13.
42. Pargiter 1911, 1913.
43. The *Ṛg Veda* is henceforth abbreviated to RV.
44. This, according to U.P. Shah (1958, p. 43), represents the assimilation of a powerful Vṛṣākapi cult by the Vedic Aryans.
45. *priyā taṣṭāni me kapir vyaktā vyadūduṣat* (10:86:5).
The above translation is by W.D.O' Flaherty in *The Rig Veda* 1981, p. 259. This may, according to Sāyaṇa, refer to the spoiling of the oblations prepared for Indrāṇī by her worshippers (*The Hymns of the Ṛgveda* 1889, note on 10:86:5), or, according to Griffith (Ibid.) and

O'Flaherty (*The Rig Veda* 1981, p. 258; p. 262, note 6), to her assault as evidenced in the following verse (10:86:6) where she describes her own sexual charms.

46. The *Brahma Purāṇa* does not derive Indrāṇī's anger from any specific action of Vṛṣākapi, but rather from her jealousy of the latter's position in regard to her husband's affections (129:100).
47. Pargiter 1911, p. 808.
48. *mārjārasaṃjñitāt tasmād dhanūmantaṃ vṛṣākapim* //
As pointed out by Söhnen and Schreiner (1989, p.149), the above is incomplete because there is no verb for the accusative masculine of *hanūmantam* and *vṛṣākapim*. The verse can be explained, however, by referring to 129:1-2a quoted in note 49 below.
49. *indratīrtham iti khyātaṃ tatraiva ca vṛṣākapam / phenāyāḥ saṃgamo yatra hanūmantaṃ tatraiva ca // abjakaṃ cāpi yat proktaṃ yatra devas trivikramaḥ /*
50. *Āṇ* means "male", and *mandi*, "monkey". See Pargiter 1913, pp. 397-98.
51. Aryans, Pargiter claims, sometimes prefixed "h" to borrowed Dravidian names (Ibid., pp. 398-99).
52. Shah 1958. Reference to Chattopadhyaya's view is found on pp.69-70 of Shah's article.
53. Shah 1958, p. 45.
54. In the *Mahābhārata* (13:135).
55. Henceforth abbreviated to Mbh.
56. Shah 1958, p. 45.
57. *Ekaśṛnga varāha* (Mbh 12:330:27).
58. Some Vedic commentators (Monier-Williams 1899) as well as Mbh 3:191 (Böhtlingk and Roth 1855-75) have also identified Vṛṣākapi with the sun. Furthermore, the *Gopatha Brāhmaṇa* (2:6:12) equates Vṛṣākapi with *āditya* (Shah 1958, p. 42).
59. Shah 1958, p. 63.
60. *The Rig Veda* 1981, p. 259.
61. In Indonesia and Thailand, the case is different. See p. 89, note 21.
62. Shah 1958, p. 45.
63. Jacobi 1893, pp. 132-33.
64. Ibid., p. 133.
65. Weber 1870, pp. 173,175.
66. Aryan, pp. 14-15.
67. See Campbell 1949, p. 30.
68. Bulcke 1959-60.
69. Crit. ed., *Yuddhakāṇḍa*, p. xxix.
70. Winternitz 1904-20, vol.1, p. 517.
71. Bulcke 1959-60, p. 393.
72. Winternitz 1904-20, vol.1, pp.496-97; crit. ed., *Yuddhakāṇḍa*, p. xxix; Bulcke 1959-60, p. 396.
73. It is generally accepted that the *Bāla* and *Uttara kāṇḍas* are later than

the rest of the epic. See Jacobi 1893, p. 64 and R.P. Goldman in *The Rāmāyaṇa of Vālmīki* : *Bālakāṇḍa* 1984, p. 15.

74. Lüders 1939, pp. 95-96.
75. Ibid., p. 95.
76. Winternitz 1904-20, vol.1, p. 516.
77. This account is given in the AdhyR (2:6:64-86).
78. Winternitz 1904-20, vol.1, p. 501.
79. Sankalia 1982, p. 98.
80. While in the Bengali *Rāmāyaṇas* he is an astrologer, in the popular belief he is the founder of astrology, as well as of a school of Indian music (Sen 1920, p. 21). Furthermore, authorship of the *Mahānāṭaka* is traditionally ascribed to him (see p. 9).
81. Bulcke 1959-60, p. 397.
82. The traditional belief amongst orthodox Hindus is that Hanumān, who is presently living in his monkey body, will be appointed as the next Brahmā (Aiyar 1951, p. 180).
83. Stages B. and C. listed on pp. 6-7.
84. According to Jacobi (1893), much of the *Sundarakāṇḍa* consists in later interpolations. Specific instances are dealt with in the scene-by-scene comparative analysis.
85. Wurm 1976, pp. 140ff.
86. E.g. 4:2:13.
87. E.g. Hanumān's slaying of Nikumbha (6:64).
    Wurm 1976 (p. 147) lists a number of instances which do not belong either to the general or to the functional pattern. All of these, however, are reflections of Hanumān's *kapitva*: no matter how noble a monkey he may be, he is still a monkey, and traces of his "monkeyness" inevitably arise every now and then. These occurrences are individually dealt with in the scene-by-scene comparative analysis.
88. Dates given range from the tenth to the thirteenth century.
89. Bhattacharya 1934; Dasgupta and De 1962, p. 505; De 1931; De 1937; Dowson 1879, p. 117; Garg 1982, p. 136; Krishnamachariar 1937, p. 640; G.S. Sastri 1943, pp. 113-14.
90. The Dāmodara recension (*Hanumannāṭaka*) has 548 verses in 14 acts, while the Madhusūdana recension (*Mahānāṭaka*) has 720 verses in 9 acts.
91. According to legend, Vālmīki was alarmed that his work would fade away before Hanumān's and therefore requested the latter's permission to throw the second into the sea. (In another version, when Hanumān heard Vālmīki was writing the epic, he feared his own composition would eclipse Vālmīki's, and thus, threw his own into the ocean.) When fragments of it were washed ashore, King Bhojā of Dhārā had the play restored.
92. Mostly verbose and sentimental verses.
93. *Uttararāmacarita, Hitopadeśa, Anargha Rāghava* etc.

94. Ghosh 1963, pp. 170ff.; Krishnamachariar 1937, p. 646.
95. Bakker 1982, pp. 106-107; McGregor 1984, p. 106.
Strictly speaking, this is not a *Rāmakathā* work, but it is mentioned here due to its importance in the development of *Rāmabhakti*.
96. *Hindu Myths* 1975, pp. 17-18.
97. Daniélou 1963 (p. 173) mentioned five in particular: *Agni Purāṇa* 5-11; *Brahma Purāṇa* 213; *Devī Bhāgavata Purāṇa* 3:28; *Kūrma Purāṇa* 1:21; *Padma Purāṇa* 4:1-68; 6:269-71. To these, *Bhāgavata Purāṇa* 9:10-12 may be added.
98. *Śiva Purāṇa* 3:20.
99. The *Adbhuta Rāmāyaṇa* claims to be the eighth (*Adbhutottara*) *kāṇḍa* of the ValR.
100. B.P. Singh's "*Bhuṣuṇḍi Rāmāyaṇa* and Its Influence on the Medieval *Rāmāyaṇa* Literature" in Raghavan 1980, pp. 475-504.
101. *Laghu-Yoga-Vāsiṣṭha* 1896, pp. vii ff.; *Kavitāvalī* 1964, p. 25.
102. Brockington 1984, p. 256; Krishnamachariar 1937, p. 22.
103. *Kavitāvalī* 1964, pp. 28-29; Krishnamachariar 1937, pp. 21-22; Shastri 1944; Whaling 1980, pp. 102,105ff.; Winternitz 1904-20, vol. 1, pp. 578-79. Its most highly cherished parts, the "Rāmagītā" (7:5) and the "Rāmahṛdaya" (1:1), are earlier than the rest of the text and still exist separately. R.G. Bhandarkar (1913, p. 48) also mentioned another "Rāmagītā", which, like the *Bhagavad Gītā,* is composed of eighteen chapters, and which is narrated by Rāma to Hanumān. This, however, is a very modern compilation.
104. Capitals are used when Rāma is considered to have divine status.
105. Grierson 1926-28; Krishnamachariar 1937, p. 21.
106. The *Rāmatāpanīya Upaniṣad* consists of two parts: the *Rāmapūrvatāpanīya*, which treats of the life of Rāma in a way reminiscent of the AdhyR, and the *Rāmottaratāpanīya*, which is a collection of pieces from various *Upaniṣads*.
107. Brockington 1984, p. 251, note 49; Daniélou 1963, pp. 173-75; Dowson 1879, p. 263; Whaling 1980, pp. 99,101; Weber 1852, p. 168.
108. Brockington 1984, p. 259 from V. Raghavan's "The *Tattvasaṃgraha Rāmāyaṇa* of Rāmabrahmānanda", (*Annals of Oriental Research* [University of Madras] 10 [1952-53], pp. 1-55). Though it extends beyond Tulasī Dāsa's time, this text is mentioned herein due to its intended wide compass.
109. KKlf, vol. 1, pp. xxxiii-xliv; Aiyangar 1942; Krishnamachariar 1937, pp. 23-26; Raghavan 1941-42; P.P.S. Sastri 1942.
Amṛtakataka by Kataka Mādhav Yogīndra (Mādhavayogin), *Tilaka* by Nāgeśa Bhaṭṭa, and *Rāmāyaṇaśiromaṇi* by Bansidhara Śivasahāya are not mentioned above because they date back to the seventeenth and the eighteenth centuries and therefore extend beyond the scope of the present study.
110. Bulcke 1959-60, p. 399.

Sen (1920, pp. 48-51) points out that the Śāktas, who portrayed Hanumān as a servant of Caṇḍī, as well as Buddhists, who in the *Śūnya Purāṇa* made him a gatekeeper as well as Buddha's minister, also wanted to share in his popularity.

111. E.g. RV 2:33:1.
112. Since then (*c*.850 C.E.), Hanumān has been and still is iconographically represented with a *vajra*. See Liebert 1976, p. 100.
113. Bulcke 1959-60, p. 399. Ghurye (1962, p. 231), however, favours a later date (after the tenth century C.E.).
114. Bulcke 1959-60, p. 399; Bulcke 1950, pp. 158, 161, 163, 203, 661-65, 667, 734.
115. Bulcke 1959-60, p. 399.
116. Vaudeville 1982, p. 6.
117. Mani 1975, p. 307.
118. Hopkins 1915, p. 14. Hanumān, like Skanda, is referred to as *śiśu*, mothered by the gods, and likened to the latter in leaping and roaring (7:35:22; 7:36:3,9). Also, both lead an army.
119. Coomaraswamy 1928-31, part 1, p. 29. All of these images date back to the first and the second centuries B.C.E.
120. Note that from here onwards, *Vinaya Patrikā*, *Dohāvalī*, and *Hanumān Bāhuka* are abbreviated to VP, D, and HB, respectively.

    The RCM does not explicitly identify Hanumān with Śiva, but at a theological level of interpretation, implicit association may be inferred from Tulasī Dāsa's verses of invocation at the beginning of each *kāṇḍa*: in the first three, Śiva (Śaṅkara, Śiva-Śaṅkara, Śaṅkara) is venerated prior to Rāma, whereas in the last four, the order is reversed, placing Rāma before Śiva (Kāśī, Hanumān, Śaṅkara, Śaṅkara). Kāśī may be understood as Śiva, for it is his city; and Hanumān may also represent Śiva, due to an otherwise established pattern of invocation and Tulasī Dāsa's acceptance of this association in his other works. The *Kiṣkindhākāṇḍa*, wherein the order is reversed, also marks the entry of Hanumān on the scene. As the servant and devotee of Rāma, Śiva (as Hanumān) is now logically subordinated to Rāma. (Based on RCM lectures by Swami Tejomayananda.)
121. Grierson 1910, p. 271.
122. Ghurye 1962, p. 233.
123. Mahipati 1932, wherein he is said to be the eleventh Rudra (2:39).
124. Bulcke 1959-60, p. 399.
125. Wolcott 1978, pp. 660-61.
126. It is to be noted that in Indonesian and Thai *Rāmakathās*, Hanumān is portrayed in a diametrically opposed light: his love-adventures are given prominence. This may stem, as Bulcke (1959-60, pp. 400-401) points out, from Bharata's gift of sixteen virgins to Hanumān (ValR 6:113:40-41).
127. *c*.700-1150 C.E. (*Hindu Myths* 1975, p. 18).

128. Bulcke 1959-60, p. 400.
129. Reference to Śaṅkarācārya's "Kaupīna Pañcaka" in *Minor Works of Śrī Śaṅkarācārya* 1952, p. 354.
130. Van der Veer 1988, p. 149.
131. Briggs 1938, pp. 12 (note 5), 17.
132. RCM 5: śl.3.
133. This may be read as a rise in stature from a mortal hero to God (Jacobi 1893, p. 61; Brockington 1984, pp. 218-25), or as the bringing to manifestation of what was potentially present in the ValR (Whaling 1980, pp. 14,82-92; S.I. Pollock in *The Rāmāyaṇa of Vālmīki : Araṇyakāṇḍa* 1991, pp. 18-19). It is the development of a human, who, according to traditional interpretation (*The Rāmāyaṇa of Vālmīki*: *Araṇyakāṇḍa* 1991, pp. 32,52 [note 112],251-52 [note on 3:4:18-19]), is not aware of his godhood, to a Self-conscious God Who plays out His humanity.
134. Grierson 1910, p. 269.
135. This becomes amply clear in the traditional accounts of Tulasī Dāsa's life. See pp.13-15.
136. Bulcke 1959-60, p. 401.
137. *Ānanda Rāmāyaṇa, Lāṅgūla Upaniṣad, Hanumatsahasranāma Stotra*, as referred to in Bulcke 1959-60, p. 401.
138. *Kavitāvalī* 1964, pp. 33,43.
139. *Bhakta Mālā* in *The Rāmāyaṇa of Tulasī Dāsa* 1978, pp. xlii-xliii; Mahipati 1933, 3:18; *Mūla Gosāin Carita* in Handoo 1964, p. 8.
140. C. Vaudeville (1955, p. 3) suggests that RCM 1: śl.4 may also imply a recognition of Hanumān as the author of the *Mahānāṭaka* in that he is being invoked together with Vālmīki, both of whom are authors of great works.
141. The Kali *yuga*.
142. See *Shri Ramacharitamanasa* 1989, p. 857.
143. Grierson 1893, pp. 206,269.
144. In his commentary on the *Bhakta Mālā* (in *The Rāmāyaṇa of Tulasī Dāsa* 1978, pp. xliii-xlvi). See also Grierson 1893, pp. 269-70; Mahipati 1933, 3:93ff.
145. *The Rāmāyaṇa of Tulasī Dāsa* 1978, pp. xliv-xlvii, Grierson 1893, p. 273; Mahipati 1933, 3:257 ff.
146. Handoo 1964, p. 47.
147. Grierson 1893, pp. 270-71.
148. The deity representing the Kali age.
149. Grierson 1893, pp. 257-58; *The Petition to Rām* 1966, pp. 39-40.
150. Eck 1983, p. 87.
151. For information on Tulasī Dāsa's writings, see Grierson 1893, pp. 89-98,122-29,197-206,225-36,253-64.

2

COMPARATIVE ANALYSIS

With a general perspective of the development of Hanumān's characterization from his origins to Tulasī Dāsa's works in mind, it is now possible to delve into a more detailed study, focusing on the ValR and the RCM. The scene-by-scene analysis is limited to the *kāṇḍas* wherein Hanumān plays the most prominent role, the *Kiṣkindhā* and the *Sundara*, with two exceptions: the bringing of the Himalayan peak to Laṅkā (*Yuddhakāṇḍa*) and the second account of Hanumān's birth and youthful exploits (*Uttarakāṇḍa*). The former episode has become so famous that it cannot be neglected, and the latter is included in the discussion of the first account of Hanumān's birth and youth (4:65:8-27). Apart from his comparatively less prominent role in the *Yuddhakāṇḍa*, another reason for not covering the scenes therein is that they present, for the most part, two characteristics of Hanumān, his fighting skills and his loyalty and service to Rāma, both of which are already amply demonstrated in the *Sundarakāṇḍa*.[1]

For the sake of simplicity and clarity, and especially due to the progression of the development of Hanumān's characterization from the *Kiṣkindhākāṇḍa* to the *Sundarakāṇḍa*,[2] the order in which the scenes are discussed is the same order in which they appear in the *Rāmakathā*. Special reference is made to the AdhyR because it is the main link between Vālmīki and Tulasī Dāsa: it sums up the tendencies within the Rāma tradition of the time (late fifteenth to early sixteenth century C.E.), adds new elements of its own, and paves the way for Tulasī Dāsa, for whom it becomes one of the main sources in writing his *magnum opus*.[3]

The arrival of Hanumān on the scene...

REFERENCES

1. The *Bāla*, *Ayodhyā*, and *Araṇya kāṇḍas* are not discussed because Hanumān does not appear therein. As for the *Uttarakāṇḍa*, other than the above mentioned scene, it contains only a few references to him.
2. See p. 8.
3. Whaling 1980, p. 102.

3

THE FIRST MEETING BETWEEN HANUMĀN AND THE RĀGHAVAS

ValR 4:2-4
RCM 4:1:1—4:4:3

The scene begins on Mount Ṛśyamūka, where a group of monkeys live in exile. Their leader Sugrīva has had a dispute with his brother Vālin, the king of the monkeys, and ever dreads that the latter is making plans to kill him. At the sight of Rāma and Lakṣmaṇa in the distance, his fears are re-ignited. In the ValR, he becomes hysterical (4:2:2-3), unable to decide what to do[1] (4:2:16). His minister Hanumān has to reassure him that Vālin is nowhere to be seen (4:2:14-15) and even to instruct him on what steps should now be taken; that is, to find out who the two men are (4:2:17).[2] In the RCM (4:1:2), on the other hand, Sugrīva is still sufficiently in his senses to dispatch Hanumān to uncover their identity without having to be told to do so. It is to be noted, however, that though the RCM presents Sugrīva in a more self-controlled light, in the ValR he is found to give far more detailed instructions to his messenger. Two conclusions may be drawn from this. The first is that Tulasī Dāsa abridges Vālmīki, and the second, that Hanumān has so successfully calmed down Sugrīva that the latter is now able to provide the minutest details in his directions—quite an achievement considering Sugrīva's mental condition just moments earlier. The second conclusion also gives the first indication of the monkey leader's relationship of dependency on Hanumān.

In prescribing such precise orders (flattery, gestures etc.), Vālmīki (4:2:23-26) allows Hanumān less leeway to manoeuvre, but as will be seen, Hanumān does not let himself be restricted by these. He is also told, though indirectly, to enlist the Rāghavas' help[3] (in overturning Vālin)—a possibility, in the RCM, which both Sugrīva and Hanumān do not yet see.

There is one way, however, in which the RCM instructions are more specific than those of the ValR: whereas Vālmīki merely states that Hanumān should take the form of an ordinary person (*prākṛta*),[4] and the latter then himself decides to come as a religious mendicant (*bhikṣu*),[5] Tulasī stipulates the guise of a *brahmacārin* (*baṭu*).[6] While Vālmīki underlines Hanumān's capacity as a thinker, a decision maker, a knower of right time and right action, Tulasī suffuses every part of his work with *Rāmabhakti*, and therefore, devotee-Sugrīva suggests the apparel of the purest of beings when appearing before the Lord.

Upon arriving before the Rāghavas, Tulasī's Hanumān bows his head (*mātha nāī*) to them (4:1:3). In the vulgate ValR, he is said to prostrate (*praṇipatya*),[7] which incident, though it reflects a recognition of Rāma's divine status, to which the commentators are by no means inimical, creates a difficulty at the temporal level: *bhikṣus* do not prostrate to householders (*gṛhasthas*). Since the ValR does not, like the later *Rāmakathās*,[8] transcend right conduct, this insertion must be aligned with the earlier layers of the text, and therefore, some of the commentators, such as Govindarāja, explain Hanumān's behaviour as a symptom of self-forgetfulness.[9]

Though in both texts (ValR 4:3:4ff.; RCM 4:1:4) Māruti is struck by their *kṣatriya* appearance and their beauty, their might and prowess are emphasized in the ValR (4:3:5-16), and their awe-inspiring attractiveness and divinity in the RCM (4:1:4-5). While Vālmīki highlights Hanumān's perceptivity and shrewdness of mind, Tulasī presents him as, above all, a devotee. Vālmīki's Hanumān immediately notices that though they are dressed as ascetics (4:3:4), their limbs (4:3:7-8,11-12), their weapons (4:3:7,14-16), and their general aura bespeaking of prowess incarnate (4:3:7-9) clearly manifest their *kṣatriya* birth and nature. Tulasī's Hanumān, following the AdhyR (4:1:13-16), also briefly notes this (RCM 4:1:4), but considers there is divinity under their external appearance (RCM 4:1:5).

The observant *saciva* sees the body and the mind, whereas the *bhakta* sees the divinity inherent in and expressing through the body and the mind.

As for the mode of questioning, Vālmīki's Māruti intersperses descriptions with questions in every second or third verse (4:3:4,6,9,12), as does Tulasī's Āñjaneya, though in a more structured manner, following the pattern of a threefold question-description (4:1:4-5)[10] and culminating in a triple question (4:1:5—4:do.1). The two basic queries are with regard to the Rāghavas' identity and their reason for being in the forest. In a general way, Hanumān has already guessed the answer of the "who" question, both at the external as well as the internal level: the *kṣatriyas* of the ValR are essentially, in the consideration of the RCM's Māruti (4:1:5—4:do.1), Nara and Nārāyaṇa, the Cause of the world (*jaga kārana*), and the Lord in human incarnation (*manuja avatāra*).

For Tulasī (4:2:1-2), following the AdhyR (4:1:17-20), this much description and questioning is sufficient to prompt the Rāghavas to reply. In the ValR, however, as they remain silent (4:3:17), Hanumān is forced to encourage them further by revealing information about himself and Sugrīva (4:3:18-21). Another possibility is that Āñjaneya, according to the *Bhūṣaṇa*, has silenced the Rāghavas by his skill in speech and is now anticipating, according to the *Tattvadīpikā*, *Tilaka*, and *Rāmāyaṇaśiromaṇi*, their questions concerning his identity.[11] The very fact that he discloses this, thereby consciously placing the monkeys in a vulnerable position, is a clear indication, since he is by no means stupid, that he does not think them to be sent by Vālin. Though Sugrīva dispatched him as a spy, it would appear that Hanumān may never have suspected them in the least, and as earlier hinted at when he was calming his master down (4:2:14-15), that he does not fear Vālin. Sugrīva seems to be suffering from paranoia, for his brother did not intend on killing him (4:16:7), and in fact, according to an inserted passage,[12] deliberately refrained from doing so when the opportunity arose.[13] Thus, from the very beginning, Hanumān's intention had been to make an alliance with the Rāghavas rather than to spy on them.[14]

Hearing that Sugrīva is also in need of help, Rāma is delighted (ValR 4:3:23), and Hanumān finally receives a response. The elder Rāghava praises Māruti the skilful speaker (*vākyajña*) whom he had been seeking to meet (4:3:24-25), as advised by the demon Kabandha (3:68:12-13), on the basis of his own and Sugrīva's mutual need (3:68:10-11). Furthermore, since Sītā has been abducted in the forest, it is clearly an advantage to have forest dwellers with special powers as allies and searchers.[15] Though at this point Hanumān does not know what the Rāghava requires, he has immediately spotted the favourable circumstance of mutual need (4:4:1-2). He seizes the opportunity by further gaining Rāma's confidence, questioning him in a solicitous and most perceptive way (4:4:4): he makes known the sharpness of his own mind by referring to Lakṣmaṇa as the younger brother (*anuja*)—information he has acquired, as Govindarāja explains,[16] from the Rāghavas' mutual resemblance (*anyonyasadṛśau*)[17] and from Rāma's instructions to Lakṣmaṇa (4:3:25). By this observation, Hanumān is indirectly hinting at the intelligence of the allies that Rāma will be gaining, thereby making an alliance with the monkeys more attractive. Lakṣmaṇa then tells Hanumān about himself, his brother, and Sītā's abduction (4:4:6-16).

In the RCM, following the AdhyR (4:1:19-20), the Rāghavas' reply to Hanumān's questions precedes the latter's introduction of himself and Sugrīva. This difference from the ValR in the order of events is significant because it represents the belief that the Lord always takes the first step towards the devotee. Furthermore, it allows Tulasī to bring in the theme of the omniscient Lord: Hanumān, having recognized Rāma, is surprised that the Latter should, like a mere mortal (*nara kī nāīṃ*), question him about what He must already know (4:2:4).

The RCM (4:2:3—4:do.3) takes great care to develop the topic of the relationship of *Bhagavān-bhakta* in the form of master-servant. It is said that Hanumān "recognized" (*pahicāni*) the Lord, thereby implying a prior acquaintance, at the very least, with Him. This is a reference, at one level, to

Brahmā's earlier command to the gods to incarnate as monkeys and serve the feet of Hari (1:do.187).[18] This the *devas* carry out and await the Lord's arrival (1:188:2). Following the Rāghavas' speech (4:2:1-2), Hanumān realizes that the waiting time is over, for Rāma is present before him. Āñjaneya falls at His feet, his body bristling, and gazes at the Lord's beautiful attire (*rucira beṣa kai racanā*).[19] At least two reasons may be given as to why Hanumān looks at Rāma's clothes rather than His face: the devotee's humility and the veneration of the incarnation of Rāma. In the latter, clothing, because it is outer, represents external manifestation—in this case, the particular form of Rāma. Though Hanumān recognizes the Lord's formless nature,[20] he is especially devoted to this one form, his chosen deity (*iṣṭadevatā*), through which the Formless expresses. When Māruti displays surprise at the Omniscient's question about his identity (4:2:4), he shifts his focus from the Lord's clothes to His face, for the eyes reflect His formless aspect. Fear arises in Hanumān when he considers that Rāma may be asking the question precisely because, in His form aspect, He has forgotten him. (Forgetfulness is not possible at the formless level because formlessness presupposes all-pervasiveness, and therefore, omniscience.) Hanumān thinks his wicked heart (*kuṭila hṛdaya*)[21] may be the cause not only for his original inability to recognize the Lord, but also for Rāma's apparent inability to recognize him. His own delusion, however, is not his fault, for it is caused by the Lord's veiling power (*māyā*) and thus requires Raghupati's grace to be removed (4:3:1). As Rāma's servant, Hanumān depends on Him in every way (4:3:2).

Again, Āñjaneya falls at the Lord's feet and finally discloses his monkey form (*nija tanu*).[22] Significantly, it is only then that he is embraced by Rāma (4:3:3), and not when he is in disguise.[23] At one level, this is an explanation for the Lord's prior apparent inability to recognize Hanumān: the Omniscient knows him as he truly is, and therefore, recognizes him as such. To acknowledge Māruti as he is not, that is, in a form which is not his own, though it would point out Rāma's omniscience, the unequivocal emphasis would be lacking, for the indication would be more like a casual warning posted on the side of the road, rather than an abrupt stop sign demanding immediate attention. At another level, the point is not so much recognition as it is embracement. Raghupati cannot unite with (embrace) His devotee so long as the latter does not remove all his masks and self-created superimpositions. As the One present in all beings, the Lord is revealed when all the outer layers are peeled off, and, emptied of accretions, the *bhakta* is found to be filled with *Bhagavān* (RCM 1:do.7c).

At this juncture, an important statement is made by the Lord: Hanumān is dearer to Him than Lakṣmaṇa (4:3:4). One possible interpretation is as follows: it is a younger brother's duty to serve his elder brother, but Hanumān, who has no blood relation or obligation to Rāma, will be doing it out of pure love and devotion. In fact, Māruti's function is far greater than Lakṣmaṇa's in that he is the means whereby all results are achieved. It is through Hanumān that the alliance between Rāma and Sugrīva is concluded (ValR 4:5; RCM 4:do.4), Sītā is found (ValR 5:13; RCM 5:8:4), and the army is brought back to life (ValR 6:61,89; RCM 6:54:4—6:62:1).[24] Were it not for Āñjaneya, Viṣṇu's promise (ValR 1:14:17—1:15:7; RCM 1:187:1-4) would remain unfulfilled. Therefore, Rāma's statement is neither surprising nor exaggerated.

Hanumān's exclusive devotion (*ananyagati*)[25] stands in clear contrast to his skill in speech (*vākyajña*).[26] Over time, the ideal *saciva* has been transformed into the ideal *bhakta*, the *ananyabhakta*.[27]

REFERENCES

1. Literally: "not fixed in thought" (*na sthāpayasi yo matau*).
2. R.J. Lefeber (KKlf) translates *iṅgitaiḥ sarvam ācara* (4:2:17) as "you must by [interpreting your enemies'] gestures do everything [necessary]", supplying the bracketed portions (the brackets are mine). Clearly, the Rāghavas' intentions, based on their identity and manifested in their *iṅgitas*, can only be examined if they are approached, and therefore, Sugrīva is being told to send a messenger/spy to them.
3. *Mamaivābhimukhaṃ sthitvā* (4:2:25) is being taken in the causative sense ("making them well disposed towards me") following Rāmānuja, Maheśvaratīrtha, and Govindarāja. See KKlf, vol. 2, note on 4:2:24-25.

4. 4:2:23.
5. 4:3:3.
6. 4:1:2.
7. Crit. ed., passage 87 inserted following 4:3:3.
8. E.g. p. 99.
9. Aiyangar 1942, p. 53.
10. Though the third one (4:1:5ab) does not actually contain an interrogative particle, the wording implies a question: *mṛdula manohara sundara gātā / sahata dusaha bana ātapa bātā //*
11. See KKlf, vol. 2, note on 4:3:18 (and also note on 4:2:24). According to the *Amṛtakataka* and the *Tilaka*, Hanumān is actually praising Sugrīva, based on the latter's orders (Kataka Mādhavayogin interpreted the "flattery" of 4:2:24 as referring to the praise of the monkey leader himself).
12. Crit. ed., *Kiṣkindhākāṇḍa*, Appendix 1, no. 14, line 29.
13. Masson 1975, p. 676.
14. Wurm 1976, p. 95.
15. KKlf, vol. 1, p. xxii. The *Uttarakāṇḍa* (7:16:13-15) attempts to give a reason for Rāma's unusual alliance by relating that Nandin cursed Rāvaṇa to be destroyed along with his relatives by monkeys.
16. Ibid., vol. 2, note on 4:4:4.
17. 4:3:10.
18. Partly as a result of Nārada's curse (1:137:3-4).
19. 4:2:3.
20. E.g. 5:21:2.
21. 4:do.2.
22. 4:3:3.
23. Based on RCM lectures by Swami Tejomayananda.
24. In the second account of the ValR (6:89) and in the RCM, Lakṣmaṇa is the only one who requires to be brought back to life.
25. RCM 4:3:4. Tulasī also uses the term *ananyamati* (4:do.3).
26. ValR 4:3:25. In the AdhyR (4:1:17), Hanumān's skill in speech is magnified to mastery of grammar (*śabdaśāstra*).
27. The term *ananyabhakta* is to be found in the *Maitri* (*Maitrāyaṇīya*) *Upaniṣad* (6:29). Furthermore, the *Bhagavad Gītā* characterizes those who worship the Lord with single-mindedness (*bhajanty ananyamanasaḥ* [9:13]) as *ananyabhāk* (9:30).

4

THE CONSOLATION OF TĀRĀ

ValR 4:21

Following the conclusion of the alliance between Rāma and Sugrīva (ValR 4:5; RCM 4:do.4), the elder Rāghava, in accordance with the terms of agreement, kills Vālin (ValR 4:16; RCM 4:do.8). Hearing the news, Vālin's wife Tārā is overcome with grief, and Hanumān tries to console her. This scene appears only in the ValR, the reason for which will be made clear upon examination of the passage.

Hanumān tells Tārā that she should not mourn because Vālin's death was a product of his *karma*, because only his physical body has been destroyed, because death and birth are ever uncertain, and because Vālin has gone to the place of the righteous (4:21:2-7). In an attempt to divert her attention from her husband, he tells her that her son Aṅgada should be looked after (4:21:4), and in fact, that the latter should be consecrated (4:21:9,11) following the performance of Vālin's last rites (4:21:10-11).

Given Hanumān's otherwise unwavering devotion to Sugrīva, his suggestion to make Aṅgada king is rather strange. Āñjaneya clearly knows, since he was instrumental in bringing about the precious alliance, that Sugrīva intends the kingdom for himself—even dying Vālin insists that it should be so (4:22:5). Only Hanumān and the hysterical monkeys (4:19:14; 4:21:9,11) suggest Aṅgada's consecration. Wise Tārā knows better than to follow this advice (4:21:13-16), and shortly thereafter, Hanumān is found to have reverted back to his position of loyalty to Sugrīva, praising Rāma for having fulfilled the latter's object (4:25:3-7).[1]

The question is: what happened in Hanumān's mind during this brief lapse? Can this slip be attributed to the fickleness of monkeys? At best, it may be argued that he was overcome with compassion at Tārā's sorrow, and in his *kapitva*, temporarily deluded as to right action. This would agree with another situation wherein, overwhelmed at Sītā's grief, he oversteps the bounds of propriety by offering to take her back himself to Rāma (5:35:21), and also, in yet another scene, to kill the *rākṣasīs* who have been tormenting her (6:101:25). However, in light of Hanumān's sharp and perceptive mind, the above explanation may be too simplistic. As a thinker, he could not have failed to notice a certain impropriety, both in the killing of Vālin and in the way he was killed. If Vālin had not actually been persecuting Sugrīva, and the latter was only being paranoid (4:2:14-15),[2] and if Vālin was indeed the legitimate king; then surely his murder was neither an act of self-defense nor a punishment for stolen kingdom. Sugrīva had absolutely no right to rule so long as his elder brother was alive. And as for the oft-quoted reason of punishment for taking Sugrīva's wife Rumā (4:18:18-20), this does not seem to have been Sugrīva's aim, for when his loyal minister and spokesman Hanumān first realized that Rāma also had need of the exiled monkey, Āñjaneya did not think to himself: "Sugrīva will get back Rumā", or "Vālin will be punished for the incest he committed", but rather "Sugrīva will get the kingdom (*rājyāgama*)",[3] for that is the objective (*kṛtya*).[4] Sugrīva himself asks Rāma to kill Vālin (4:12:11). It may also be suggested that he exhibits this desire for power, though perhaps at a subconscious level, when he blocks the entrance of the cave wherein his brother and the demon Māyāvin are engaged in battle: as blood comes flowing forth, he automatically assumes that Vālin has been killed.[5] However, it is hardly conceivable how the mighty monkey king could have failed to defeat Māyāvin (who, in fact, ran away from him [4:9:9]) when he succeeded in overcoming the latter's father Dundubhi, whose huge body was the size of Mount Kailāsa, who had the strength of one thousand elephants (4:11:7), and with whom even the Ocean (4:11:11) and Himālaya (4:11:17) would not fight.

By forming an alliance with Sugrīva, Rāma involves himself in the monkey's power struggle. In his humanity,[6] the Rāghava does actually "need" Sugrīva's help in finding Sītā. Furthermore, due to the loss of his own spouse, he immediately responds to the exiled monkey who is in the same predicament and with whom, consequently, he feels certain bonds.[7] Therefore, he does not stop to question the righteousness of the cause: at the same time as he is asking for details concerning the enmity between Vālin and Sugrīva (4:8:40), he has already decided on Vālin's guilt (4:8:43).[8] The latter is killed from behind a tree, without warning, when he is fighting Sugrīva. The manner in which this is carried out only serves to underline the extent to which Rāma is willing to go in order to secure the monkeys' aid.

If Hanumān is aware of all this, which as the ideal *saciva* he undoubtedly is, his mental anxiety is to be expected. At one level, there is the remorse for being part and parcel of the plot to kill an innocent monkey king and also thereby cause grief to others. When his nobler instincts take over, he tries to alleviate his feeling of guilt by suggesting that Aṅgada be crowned. Of course, it is too late to turn back the tide, and everyone knows it.

At another level, there is the gradual and eventually climactic realization that he may have misjudged the character of the person with whom he has brought about Sugrīva's alliance. If Rāma is capable of killing Vālin in such a way, who knows what he could do to the rest of the monkeys and what he could expect from them? Panic sets in as Hanumān considers the possibilities and his own instrumentality and therefore responsibility for the alliance. It is understandable that in such a state his *kapitva* may have led him to make an inappropriate suggestion to Tārā. When he does regain control of himself, it becomes obvious that the only option open to the monkeys is to carry out quickly the terms of the agreement. Hanumān, however, may be the only one, or one of the few, who is fully aware of the seriousness of the situation.

Clearly, by the time of the AdhyR and the RCM, Māruti's advice to crown Aṅgada, as well as the implications behind this statement, is unacceptable. Rāma, as the Supreme God, is neither desperate for anyone's help nor ruthless in his actions, and therefore, never gives the ideal *bhakta* Hanumān any reason to doubt Him. Consequently, later texts omit this scene.

REFERENCES

1. Srinivas Sastri (1949, p. 263) considers this to be a failure in Hanumān's diplomacy. This suggestion seems somewhat unsound since Vālmīki never intended to have Hanumān convince Tārā, for that would drastically change the story. Āñjaneya's failure is less in diplomacy than the temporary lack thereof.
2. See p. 27. Note also the *Rāmāyaṇaśiromaṇi*'s comment on *laghucittatā* (4:2:16): "fearfulness without cause" (KKlf, vol. 2, note on 4:2:16).
3. 4:4:2.
4. Ibid.
5. J.M. Masson (1975, p. 677) makes this point, though from a different angle. In Sugrīva's own words, it is a "stream" (*vega*) of blood which flows out of the cave (4:45:6): surely such a "stream" would be more appropriate to a giant demon and his followers (4:10:20 of the Nirṇayasāgar Press edition with the *Tilaka* commentary) than to lone Vālin.
6. Whether one accepts, at least in the crit. ed. of the *Kiṣkindhākāṇḍa*, that Rāma is a mortal, or whether one takes the view that he is unaware of his divinity, as presented in ValR 6:105:10 and upheld by the traditional interpretation of the text (see *The Rāmāyaṇa of Vālmīki: Araṇyakāṇḍa* 1991, pp. 32, 52 [note 112], 251-52 [note on 3:4:18-19]), it is his humanity which is emphasized herein.
7. Masson 1975, p. 673. Therefore, the killing of Vālin becomes an outlet for Rāma's burning anger arisen from the pain of his separation from Sītā, for the similarity of his own and Sugrīva's situation makes the identification of the two psychologically possible, and the scene then serves to foreshadow the battle with Rāvaṇa.
8. Masson 1975, pp. 673-74.

5

HANUMĀN'S REMINDER TO SUGRĪVA

ValR 4:28
RCM 4:19:1-3

Sugrīva is consecrated (ValR 4:25; RCM 4:do.11) and instructed by Rāma to begin the search for Sītā after the rainy season (ValR 4:25:15; RCM 4:12:4-5). While the Rāghavas settle in a cave on Mount Prasravaṇa (ValR 4:26:1-5; RCM 4:12:5), Sugrīva enjoys himself in the city of Kiṣkindhā, forgetting all about his promise (ValR 4:28:2-6; RCM 4:18:2). Fortunately, Hanumān, who is ever keenly alert, brings the task at hand to his attention.

In both texts, this scene displays Āñjaneya's vigilance, perception, and loyalty to Sugrīva. He is mindful of the latter's duty in Rāma's purpose, as also the urgency of the work (ValR 4:28:15). In the face of Sugrīva's sensuality (ValR 4:28:2-6; AdhyR 4:4:47)—a topic which Tulasī Dāsa carefully avoids by restricting it to brief admissions (RCM 4:19:2; 4:20:4)—Hanumān realizes that the problem is not lack of good will.[1] The RCM also brings out the eternal *brahmacārin's* purity of mind by circumventing any direct accusations, condemnations, or descriptions of Sugrīva's behaviour.

Hanumān's loyalty to the monkey king differs in nature from one text to the other. In the ValR it is prompted by genuine affection and concern for Sugrīva, in this case extended to fear for him and all the monkeys due to Āñjaneya's doubts concerning Rāma. In the RCM, however, the relationship changes because Hanumān is not so much Sugrīva's messenger (*dūta*) as Rāma's, for which purpose he has taken birth. His primary concern, therefore, is to have the Lord's work done. This does not mean, however, that Māruti has no feelings for the monkey king. On the contrary, his bond with Raghupati strengthens his already existing formal as well as emotional ties with Sugrīva: when the Lord blesses and helps Sugrīva, Hanumān's love for the latter grows, for the devotee cherishes him whom the Master holds dear. For love of Rāma, Hanumān loves Sugrīva, much as Yājñavalkya in the *Bṛhadāraṇyaka Upaniṣad* (2:4:5) explains to his wife Maitreyī that "Verily, not for the sake of the beings . . . are the beings loved, but they are loved for the sake of the Self."[2] Also, the relationship between the monkeys gains an added dimension in that Āñjaneya is now concerned for Sugrīva's spiritual well-being. Therefore, though both texts uphold a concern for duty, in the ValR, Hanumān's reminder is motivated by fear, whereas in the RCM it is inspired by love (for Rāma as well as Sugrīva).

Vālmīki's Hanumān, however worried he may be, cannot present his case openly because, as noted earlier, Sugrīva is not able to function effectively in stressful situations. In an attempt to protect him, Āñjaneya uses different arguments to prompt him to action. He begins with duty, right action (*kārya*)[3] which must be performed at the right time (*kāla*),[4] for if it is the wrong time, it is also the wrong action. The appointed time is passing (4:28:14),[5] and Rāma is in a hurry (*tvaramāṇa*).[6] Furthermore, the Rāghava has already fulfilled his end of the agreement to the fullest extent (4:28:17,22). Hanumān then suggests that the delay may be mitigated by immediately mobilizing armies (4:28:17-18), thereby transforming what was on the verge of becoming the wrong time into the right time by performing the right action.

Upon careful examination of Hanumān's speech, his doubts concerning Rāma can be seen to re-surface. First, he appeals to duty. It may be deduced that since he continues to give further arguments, either he has not received from Sugrīva the response he desired for, or, overcome with fear, he wishes to emphasize his point, not recognizing that the monkey king has, at least in part, understood. In the first case, Sugrīva, overcome with sensuousness and therefore oblivious to duty, may have failed to react altogether. In the second case, Hanumān, well aware of the monkeys nature and Sugrīva's weakness in particular, coupled with his partly blinding fear of Rāma, may have projected unto the monkey king a more infatuated condition than is actually the case. By means of such a projection, Hanumān provides an outlet for himself to express, though in a concealed manner, his doubts about Rāma. The only way he can do this without alarming Sugrīva too much is by emphasizing the urgency of the situation.

Thus, when appeal to duty fails, Hanumān begins to work at the emotional level, for this is certainly more familiar to monkeys than reason or *dharma*. By telling Sugrīva that Rāma is in a hurry, he is contrasting each of their situations: while the king of the monkeys has gotten back his wife Rumā (4:25:38) and now also has Tārā (4:28:4), the Rāghava is still separated from Sītā. Given Sugrīva's attachment to women, and wise Tārā in particular, if he is not completely wrapped up in selfishness, he should be able to sympathize with Rāma. However, since the minimal amount of compassion aroused in the monkey king is not enough to compel him to act, Hanumān points out that Rāma risked his life for him (4:28:22). While it is true that it was a risk for the Rāghava to go against so powerful an adversary as Vālin,[7] he certainly did not do it out of special affection for Sugrīva, as Āñjaneya would have the latter believe.[8] Hanumān is thereby changing a business transaction into a personal favour so as to evoke in the monkey king, if not gratefulness, then at least a sense of pride that a mere monkey as himself could be considered worthy of friendship by a human. This appears to be sufficient instigation, for Sugrīva now follows Māruti's advice (4:28:18) and orders that armies be mobilized (4:28:28-32).

In the RCM, Hanumān's encouragement of Sugrīva takes an altogether different form. Out of love, he admonishes and gently, though firmly, persuades the king of the monkeys, employing all the four means (*cārihu bidhi*) to bring him round (4:19:1). According to commentators[9]: by conciliation (*sāma*) he enunciates the moral obligation towards friends and allies; by gift (*dāna*) he explains that Sugrīva owes everything to Rāma, and if, when he did nothing, he received the kingdom and his wife, then how much more will come to him by serving the Lord; by dissension (*bheda*) he argues that Rāma could win over Aṅgada and use him as a tool to dethrone Sugrīva; by force (*daṇḍa*) he points out that, as a warrior, the king of the monkeys is no match for the Rāghava, Who could punish him, even as He has done to Vālin.

In the ValR, followed by the AdhyR, *sāma* (ValR 4:28:9,12,17,19,22,24; AdhyR 4:4:44-45), *dāna* (ValR 4:28:10-11; AdhyR 4:4:46), as well as *daṇḍa* (ValR 4:28:21,23; AdhyR 4:4:48)[10] are already made use of. There is, however, a substantial difference in the degree of the *daṇḍa* employed in the texts: while Vālmīki's Hanumān never directly threatens Sugrīva, emphasizing rather Rāma's fearlessness in regard to all classes of beings and mentioning, at most, fearless Rāma's patience with the monkey king,[11] the AdhyR's Māruti does not hesitate to point directly at the potential of Sugrīva's meeting the same end as Vālin, as does, according to the commentators, Tulasī's Āñjaneya. Since Hanumān does not want to upset the ValR's Sugrīva, his arguments are much milder and the latter's consequent reaction quite calm. In the AdhyR and the RCM, because Sugrīva is seen in a better light, the admonitions can be stronger, but they also evoke a stronger response (AdhyR 4:4:49-50; RCM 4:19:2), both in his emotional condition (fear-filled), as well as in his competent intellectual resolution quickly to make amends (independent decision and order to mobilize the monkey armies). In contrasting the two Sugrīvas, the weight of the responsibility borne almost exclusively on the shoulders of Vālmīki's Hanumān, along with the latter's remarkable fortitude, is strikingly brought to light.

REFERENCES

1. Wurm 1976, p. 98.
2. *na vā are bhūtānāṃ kāmāya bhūtāni priyāṇi bhavanti ātmanas tu kāmāya bhūtāni priyāṇi bhavanti.* Translation by Swami Nikhilananda in *The Upaniṣads* 1949-59, vol. 3, p. 176.
3. 4:28:12,14.
4. 4:28:15,18.
5. Though *kālātīta* literally means "whose time has passed", the *Tilaka* supplies "it will be", for that is the sense implied by subsequent verses (KKlf, vol. 2, note on 4:28:14).

6. 4:28:15.
7. R.J. Lefeber suggests that Rāma killed Vālin, who had inordinate strength, in the only possible way he could (KKlf, vol. 1, pp. xvi-xvii).
8. The bonds, mentioned on p. 35, which Rāma feels with Sugrīva have nothing to do with affection directed specifically to the monkey, for their connection is based on the similarity of their individual situations, and therefore the Rāghava would automatically respond to anyone in the same predicament. Thus, in the early ValR, Rāma's relationship to Sugrīva is purely functional and completely impersonal.
9. The following interpretation is based on the note to RCM 4:19:1 in *Sri Ramacharitamanasa* 1949-51, and on the lectures of Swami Tejomayananda.
10. ValR 4:28:21, which expresses Rāma's ability to subdue gods, demons, and great snakes, directly contradicts the following verse (4:28:22), where Hanumān claims that the latter has risked his life for Sugrīva. Though this discrepancy may be accounted for by the different layers of the text, it clearly brings out Āñjaneya's relentless efforts to convince the monkey king in any which way possible, as well as Sugrīva's agitated condition of mind on the one hand, and his blind dependency on Māruti on the other, in that he fails to notice the contradiction in Hanumān's speech.
11. There is also the mention of Rāma's immeasurable might (4:28:16). On a more threatening note, a clearly later verse inserted following 4:28:12 (see crit. ed.) guarantees disaster for one who fails to place the concerns of his allies before his own.

6

LAKṢMAṆA'S ARRIVAL IN KIṢKINDHĀ

ValR 4:31
RCM 4:20:1-5

While Hanumān has finally succeeded in convincing Sugrīva to give orders, if nothing else, in preparation for the search for Sītā; on Mount Prasravaṇa, Rāma is loosing patience and finally sends Lakṣmaṇa to Kiṣkindhā (4:29).[1] At the news of the young Rāghava's arrival (4:30), Vālmīki's Sugrīva denies he has done anything wrong (4:31:3), claiming instead that his enemies have reported untrue faults of his (4:31:4). Obviously, Hanumān's earlier reminder has had very little effect on him, and now that danger is at his doorstep, his characteristic inability to deal with situations, thoughts, and feelings which could cause him anxiety resurfaces in the form of a defensive-offensive mechanism. In the end, frightened and confused, he only says that he cannot pay Rāma back anyway (4:31:8). As usual, Hanumān comes to the rescue, urging Sugrīva that this is the right time for right action. However, the right action, which, of course, must be spelt out for the monkey king, is not very pleasant. Since Lakṣmaṇa is fully aware of Sugrīva's inattentiveness (4:31:15), which negligence is an offence (*aparādha*),[2] the latter must propitiate the young Rāghava (4:31:17) and bow his head to Rāma (4:31:21), no matter how humiliating that may be for a king.[3] As the situation has gotten out of hand, Hanumān can no longer completely shield the monkey king. In order to impress on Sugrīva the extreme urgency involved herein, Āñjaneya draws out all the artillery, including *daṇḍa*: "when he is angered, Rāghava can, by raising his bow, bring under his control the whole world with its gods, demons, and *gandharvas*."[4] If this overzealous remark is not construed as a later interpolation reflecting Rāma's divine status, it unmistakably expresses Hanumān's own fearful disposition towards the Rāghava. Though he may be going too far in frightening Sugrīva, for he risks pushing the unstable monkey king to the point of psychological dismemberment, wherein the latter would lose all capacity to function, his concern for the safety of all the monkeys renders his action justifiable rather than rash or cruel.

Tulasī's Sugrīva, on the other hand, requires no such counselling, for he knows what to do. In all the texts, specific characters take on the role of his protective shields against Lakṣmaṇa's anger: in the ValR (4:34), Tārā volunteers; in the AdhyR (4:5:33-56), Sugrīva sends Aṅgada, Hanumān, and Tārā; and in the RCM (4:20:2-3) he sends Hanumān and Tārā. In this function there is a clear gradual enhancement of Āñjaneya's position at Tārā's cost. While Vālmīki's Hanumān pushes Sugrīva into the situation, in the RCM he acts as his buffer. In other words, originally Āñjaneya operates from behind and then from the front. This may be read as an improvement in Sugrīva's character, whereby his temperament shifts from that of the passive agent driven by Hanumān to that of the active agent who uses Āñjaneya as a channel through which to function. In the latter situation, the logic is as follows: since Māruti was Sugrīva's means to make an alliance with Rāma, he may now be the means to redeem that same alliance. When the wavering monkey unites with the eternal *brahmacārin*, the symbol of self-control and the semi-divine middleman between the Lord and the devotee, his devotion to Raghupati is steadied, and he never again, in the RCM, falls to passion.

As for the means whereby Hanumān handles Lakṣmaṇa's anger (RCM 4:20:2-3), it is through their mutual devotion to Rāma. In fact, it may be said that Tulasī's Māruti, as the very embodiment of *Rāmabhakti*, deals with any and every circumstance by bringing to manifestation his overflowing love for the Lord. In this particular case, he softens up Lakṣmaṇa by recounting Raghupati's glory (*prabhu sujasa*).[5] When the younger Rāghava no longer has the ability to feel anger, Āñjaneya pleads Sugrīva's case. So when the monkey king finally confronts Lakṣmaṇa, the latter embraces him (4:20:3).

REFERENCES

1. As the spokesman of Rāma's aggressive urges, it is appropriate that Lakṣmaṇa should be sent to Sugrīva. See Goldman 1980.
2. 4:31:17.
3. KKlf, vol. 2, note on 4:31:17.
4. *abhikruddhaḥ samartho. . . cāpam udyamya rāghavaḥ / sadevāsura-gandharvaṃ vaśe sthāpayituṃ jagat //* (4:31:19).
   Translation by R.J. Lefeber in KKlf. See also 4:31:22.
   Note how much more forceful this statement is in comparison with Hanumān's earlier use of *daṇḍa* (4:28:21,23). See p. 40.
5. 4:20:2.

7

THE SINGLING OUT OF HANUMĀN

ValR 4:43
RCM 4:23:5-6

Once the frictions between the Rāghavas and Sugrīva have been smoothed away and the monkey army has been mobilized, the monkey king organizes the search parties and dispatches them to the various regions of the earth (ValR 4:39-42; RCM 4:22:3—4:23:4). One particular group, consisting of Aṅgada, Nīla, Hanumān, and Jāmbavān, is noted as the most promising. They are sent to the south because that is where Rāvaṇa is said to live (ValR 4:40; RCM 4:23:1-4).[1] The description of the quarters (*digvarṇana*), however, is considered to be a later interpolation reflecting the balladists' tendency to expand the *Rāmakathā*.[2] In the original, according to H. Jacobi, only Hanumān was instructed to look for Sītā.[3]

In the ValR (4:43:1-6), Sugrīva singles out Āñjaneya, through whom, he feels, his object will be accomplished:

> Neither on earth, nor in the air, nor in the sky, nor in heaven, nor in the waters do I see any obstacle to your passage, bull among monkeys . . . .Nor is there another being on earth equal to you in power. Therefore you alone must bring about Sītā's recovery.[4]

His hyperbolic praise of Māruti demonstrates not only the high esteem in which he holds him, but especially his childlike perception of Hanumān as an all-powerful adult, father figure, and hero, on whom he is totally dependent. Herein is the first indication of Āñjaneya's strength (*bala*) and prowess (*parākrama*), which become so dominant in the *Sundarakāṇḍa*.

When Rāma hears Sugrīva's formidable valuation of his minister, he understands from it and from his own previous dealings with Hanumān that the latter, to whom the enterprise is being entrusted, can be relied upon (4:43:7-9). He therefore gives him his signet ring as a token of recognition for Sītā (4:43:11).

In order to emphasize the Lord's omniscient aspect, Tulasī omits Sugrīva's singling out of Hanumān so as not to give the impression that Rāma chooses him, even partly, on the basis of the monkey king's judgement. Raghupati does not require advice, instruction, or information, for, as the Indweller of all beings,[5] His knowledge of Āñjaneya is more immediate, intimate, and profound than anyone else's. "I know everything about you", says Rāma in the AdhyR, "[just] as it truly is."[6] He recognizes Hanumān as His servant, incarnated for the express purpose of doing His work and marked for success in the search for Sītā (RCM 4:23:5).

In the transfer of the ring to Āñjaneya (RCM 4:23:5), Tulasī takes the opportunity to illustrate the highly intimate and personal relationship between the Lord and the devotee. Rāma lovingly strokes Hanumān's head (4:23:5), and as opposed to the ValR, gives him instructions to comfort Sītā (4:23:6). The deeply caring and special bond that Raghupati has with each and every character in the RCM[7] stands in stark contrast to the Rāma-Sugrīva business transaction of the early ValR.

The stroking of Hanumān's head may imply more than an expression of love: as a blessing for the successful outcome of the undertaking, it is, by extension, a form of empowerment. Through touch, Rāma's *śakti* is transferred to Māruti, who is now supplied with the necessary power or energy to fulfil the difficult and also divine task. At one level, the work of the gods requires the *śakti* of the gods. This understanding brings to light yet another point: if Hanumān does Rāma's work (*Rāmakāja*) through Rāma's *śakti*, then is it not Rāma Himself Who does His own work? One may be led to analyze the compound *rāmakārya* not only as *rāmasya kārya* (the work *of* Rāma) and *rāmāya kārya* (the work *for* Rāma), but also as *rāmeṇa kārya* (the work to be done *by* Rāma). Hanumān then becomes the perfect instrument: in virtue of his total humility and therefore complete "emptiness" of ego, he provides the

Lord with "space" to accommodate His *śakti* so that He Himself may fulfil His own purpose through him.

As for the ring itself, its presence in the ValR indicates that it is a later interpolation because signet rings were introduced in North Western India only after the first century B.C.E.[8] Further evidence may be drawn from the text itself, wherein the ring is given not to Aṅgada, who is the official leader of the southern expedition (4:40:5), but to Hanumān, "the favourite son of later times".[9] Moreover, according to L.A. van Daalen,[10] the few references to the ring that appear in the *Kiṣkindhā* and *Sundara kāṇḍas*, apart from having uncertain authenticity, show irregularities of language. It should also be noted that the Mbh's *Rāmopākhyāna* has no reference whatsoever to the ring.

Obviously, the commentators have had more than a little difficulty explaining why Rāma, who was supposed to have renounced all wealth, should have a ring. In his devotional outlook, Govindarāja suggests that the Omniscient kept this one item precisely for the purpose for which it is now being used.[11]

In the RCM there is, of course, no question as to the authenticity of the ring (*mudrikā*) transference. At this stage, it has gained such prominence and developed so much symbolism that it has become essential to the story. The significance of the ring may be classified under two broad headings: the passport to Sītā and the contact between Rāma and Sītā. As the passport, it is advance notice of the mission's assured success. It is also the means of transportation to Laṅkā, as well as Sītā's dwelling therein, and the instrument for the removal of obstacles on the way by virtue of its inscription of Rāma's Name (*Rāmanāma*). When, in Tulasī Dāsa's *Gītāvalī*,[12] Hanumān receives the *mudrikā* from Raghupati, he kisses it (G 5:1)[13] and thereby imprints the Lord's Name on his lips. This is further elaborated in the *Hanumān Cālīsā*, a later text traditionally ascribed to Tulasī Dāsa, wherein Māruti actually holds the ring in his mouth throughout his flight across the ocean, and presumably until he gives it to Sītā.[14] "If you would have light within and without", says the RCM, "place the luminous Name of Rāma on your tongue, like a jewelled lamp on the threshold of the door . . ."[15]

Rāmanāma is the power, the *śakti*, which makes everything possible for Hanumān. When the vast ocean of transmigration (*saṃsāra*) can be crossed over by calling to mind the Name of the Lord, points out the AdhyR (5:1:4-5), then how insignificant is this small ocean for one who holds the *Rāmanāma mudrikā*.

The ring, as passport, introduces Hanumān to Sītā in that it is testimonial to his sincerity and proof of his identity. Seeing it, Vaidehī will know that he truly is Rāma's messenger.

The second heading, contact between Rāma and Sītā, includes the initial contact, which will eventually lead to reunion,[16] and also, more generally, communication between the Rāghava and his spouse. Through the ring, Rāma speaks to Sītā, as can be clearly observed in the G (5:3-4),[17] wherein there is an actual conversation between Vaidehī and the *mudrikā*, and it is the ring itself which points out Hanumān to Sītā (passport function). This intimate dialogue highlights Māruti's total humility, without which he would be an intruder listening in on a private conversation. In using Hanumān as a vehicle, Rāma is functioning through the perfect instrument, which in its complete surrender disappears altogether, and the Lord alone is present. It is therefore not surprising that Tulasī likens Āñjaneya to *Rāmanāma* (RCM 1:27:4), for in a sense, he is *Rāmanāma* and he is also Rāma.

It is important to understand not only Raghupati's supremacy in doing His own work, but also Hanumān's equally significant supremacy in allowing Rāma to do that work. Were it not for the instrument, the purpose of the gods would remain unaccomplished. From this point of view, it may be questioned whether Rāma is greater, or the devotee (D 111),[18] and the crow Bhuṣuṇḍi's option for the latter need not come as such a surprise (RCM 7:120:8).

Hanumān's reaction to the receipt of the ring varies greatly from one text to the other. In the ValR (4:43:14) he touches it to his head and bows at Rāma's feet, while in the RCM (4:23:6) he considers his birth fulfilled. Vālmīki's Hanumān is being polite, doing the right action at the right time, and given his doubts about Rāma, probably feeling considerably weighed down by the responsibility laid upon him. If he fails, all the monkeys will pay for the alliance he himself has single-handedly brought about. In the RCM, however, duty shifts to devotion, and fear to gratitude. Apart from being so fortunate as to be able to carry out the purpose of his monkey incarnation, he is now being given an especially important role in the task. This is an honour, but not the kind which arouses pride. Rather, as the other side of the equation, it is pride transmuted into humble gratefulness. He is not being recognized for what is of value in him, but for what is of value in Rāma; that is, Raghupati's love and compassion. The work he is being given is not a burden, but a precious gift, an opportunity to serve the Lord more actively than he had expected. Tulasī thus shifts the focus from Hanumān to Rāma so that praise of others becomes praise of Raghupati. Māruti merely serves as a pointer to draw attention to the Lord.

In short, the scene of the singling out of Hanumān provides the reader with considerable information about Āñjaneya, Sugrīva, and Rāma, as well as Māruti's relationships with the other two. Naturally, there is a great deal of difference between the Vālmīki and Tulasī versions, based on the varying perceptions of Rāma and the consequently varying attitudes of Hanumān to him. On the one hand, Āñjaneya's position as an independent character is decreased, for he is defined purely in relation to and in terms of his instrumentality for Rāma, and on the other hand, his stature increases, for the Lord of all creation depends on him.

REFERENCES

1. For a discussion of the monkeys' and Rāma's knowledge of Rāvaṇa's dwelling place, see Goldman and Masson 1969.
2. Jacobi's arguments concerning the interpolation of the *digvarṇana* center around the geographical problems and the presence of Rāma's signet ring. See Jacobi 1893, pp. 37,39.

3. Jacobi 1893, p. 39.
4. *na bhūmau nāntarikṣe vā nāmbare nāmarālaye / nāpsu vā gatisaṃgaṃ te paśyāmi haripuṃgava // . . . tejasā vāpi te bhūtaṃ samaṃ bhuvi na vidyate / tad yathā labhyate sītā tat tvam evopapādaya //* (4:43:2,5). Translation by R.J. Lefeber in KKlf. This sentiment is echoed by the monkeys of the eastern and western expeditions when they return without having found Sītā (4:46:14).
5. E.g. RCM 1:do.7c.
6. *jānāmi sattvaṃ te sarvaṃ* (4:6:29).
7. See, for instance, the scene of the return of the Rāghavas with Sītā to Ayodhyā, wherein Rāma greets each of the citizens individually (7:6:3).
8. The Indo-Greeks, who ruled Taxila and North Western India in the latter part of the second and the early part of the first century B.C.E., originally introduced the signet rings. See Sankalia 1973 (p. 56) and 1982 (p. 77).
9. L.A. van Daalen (*Vālmīki's Sanskrit* [1980], pp.141-42) referred to in KKlf, vol.1, p. lxix, note 59.
10. Ibid.
11. KKlf, vol.2, note on 4:43:11. Govindarāja also suggests that Rāma took the ring from Sītā as a love-token some time prior to Rāvaṇa's arrival, that it was the regional custom to wear a seal-ring on the little finger as a sign of affection for one's wife, or that Janaka gave it to Rāma as a wedding gift.
12. Henceforth abbreviated to G.
13. In the Bahadur translation (*Complete Works of Goswami Tulsidas* 1978-80, vol.3), see 5:219.
14. *Hanumān Cālīsā* (19). The text together with the Hindi and the English translations is to be found in *Shri Ramacharitamanasa* 1989, Appendix B, pp. 849-52.
15. *rāma nāma manidīpa dharu jīha deharīṃ dvāra / . . . bhītara bāharahuṃ jauṃ cāhasi ujiāra //* (1:do.21).
    Translation by R.C. Prasad in *Shri Ramacharitamanasa* 1989.
16. In Tulasī's case it is only apparent "reunion" because the Sītā who has been abducted is Māyā-Sītā, and not the real Sītā. See RCM 3:24:1-2.
17. In the Bahadur translation (*Complete Works of Goswami Tulsidas* 1978-80, vol. 3), see 5:221-22.
18. In the Bahadur translation (*Complete Works of Goswami Tulsidas* 1978-80, vol.1), see D 102. In this case, Tulasī is referring specifically to Hanumān, who has made the Lord indebted to him: *tulasī rāmahu teṃ adhika rāmabhakta jiya jāna / riniyā rājā rāma bhe dhanika bhae hanumāna //* Similarily, Kabīr asks: "Is Ram bigger or the knower of Ram?" (*Bījak, śabda* 112 in Kabir 1983, p. 78).

8

HANUMĀN'S PERSUASION OF AṄGADA

ValR 4:53

The monkeys, as instructed by Sugrīva, set out in the various directions. The southern expedition, though in the ValR (4:40:5) it is supposed to be under the leadership of Aṅgada, is guided by Hanumān (e.g.4:48:22). Following a vigorous search (ValR 4:47-48; RCM 4:do.23—4:24:1), an adventure in a cave (ValR 4:49-52; RCM 4:24:2—4:25:3) leads them one step closer to Laṅkā; that is, the seashore (ValR 4:52:14; RCM 4:25:3). The time limit set by Sugrīva (ValR 4:39:62; RCM 4:22:4) has now expired (ValR 4:52:15; RCM 4:26:1), and as they stand before the raging ocean, depression sets in. When Aṅgada suggests fasting unto death (ValR 4:52:21),[1] he is advised, both in the ValR (4:52:31-32) and then in the AdhyR (4:7:9-10), to return to the magic hole. While Vālmīki's Aṅgada agrees (4:52:33), the AdhyR does not give him the chance to react because Hanumān immediately cuts in (4:7:10-11), and following the ValR (4:53), proceeds to convince him not to pursue this line of action (4:7:12-22).

Tulasī Dāsa curtails this scene, carefully avoiding any suggestion that Aṅgada would even as much as consider setting up a rival kingdom in the cave. To a *Rāmabhakta*, death is preferable to self-serving actions and ends,however temporarily dejected he may happen to be.

Vālmīki, on the other hand, takes this opportunity to bring forth Aṅgada's doubts and fears concerning Sugrīva. Vālin's son must undoubtedly be aware of the unrighteousness, both in the intent and the means, of his father's murder. Furthermore, Aṅgada is the one who should have been king, and not Sugrīva.[2] Seeing that the latter is power-hungry and will do anything to achieve his purpose,what guarantee is there that he will not also kill Aṅgada,either as part of his rivalry with

Vālin, or in the hope of putting someone else[3] on the throne, or even in suspicion, due to his characteristic paranoia, that Aṅgada is trying to overthrow him. It may well be that Sugrīva's fear of Vālin has been transferred, in the form of distrust, to the latter's son, who is a constant reminder of the murder as well as a possible threat.

Hanumān surely must know that Aṅgada has more than good reason to feel victimized and even endangered, and thus, probably suspects the latter's desire for revenge on Sugrīva as well as Rāma, whose contract he could not possibly be inclined to uphold. Not only has the alliance brought about the death of his father, but his lecherous and power-craving uncle has taken his mother and his throne—he himself was made crown prince only on Rāma's insistence (4:25:11). And now, after Aṅgada has lost everything, he is being expected to honour the agreement of the one who killed his father, and in fact, to make the payment for all of Sugrīva's unrighteous gains, which consist entirely of his own personal tragic losses. However horrible this prospect may be, it is, nonetheless, completely in accordance with Vālin's last wishes,[4] which Aṅgada has thus far been following, successfully suppressing an ever-increasing sense of injustice done to him and his family, along with the accompanying feelings of anger and humiliation, and perhaps even realizing that his father's actual intention[5] may have been to save the lives of his son and his wife. When faced with the additional crisis of failure in the search for Sītā and the potential consequences thereof, it becomes more than he can bear. He loses control of himself, and all his misgivings come pouring forth (4:52:22-26).

Though Hanumān's sympathies are probably with Aṅgada, his loyalty is to Sugrīva, and his ultimate responsibility is to all the monkeys, whom he must guide to the fulfilment of their side of the alliance.If Aṅgada now sets up a rival kingdom in the cave, he will be playing against Sugrīva, and all the *vānaras* may, in the end, pay with their lives for not having found Sītā. Therefore, Hanumān's concern for the survival of the monkeys supercedes his concern for the one monkey. On the other hand, his consideration for all includes his consideration for the one. Aṅgada's survival can only be made possible by the discovery of Vaidehī. If his intention is to establish a rival kingdom in the cave, then Sugrīva and his powerful ally will surely destroy it. If he only wants to hide, Rāma will certainly find him.

In order to convince Aṅgada, Hanumān employs the four means: by *sāma* he tries to persuade him that Sugrīva is not against him (4:53:20-21); by *dāna* he suggests that if they all return, Sugrīva will give him the kingship (4:53:19); by *bheda* he causes dissension amongst the monkeys and warns that, fickle as they are, they will not remain with him (4:53:6, 9-11,15-16); and by *daṇḍa* he tries to frighten Aṅgada with threats of Lakṣmaṇa's arrows, which can easily split the cave (4:53:13-14,18).

The arguments given in the AdhyR (4:7:12-22) vary greatly from the above, for *bhakti* (devotion to the incarnation of Rāma) and *jñāna* (knowledge of Rāma as *Brahman*) are at issue. *Sāma* (Rāma loves you more than He loves Lakṣmaṇa), *bheda* (the monkeys will not stay with you), and *daṇḍa* (Rāma's arrows will penetrate everywhere) are used, in addition to an exposition of Rāma's supreme nature and a revelation, or reminder, of the monkeys' identity (residents of Vaikuṇṭha) and purpose in taking such a birth (service of Rāma), both of which may be taken as extensions of *sāma*. Clearly, some of these points follow the ValR, but the emphasis has shifted to the Rāghava, leaving behind the concern of Sugrīva's feelings for Aṅgada and the power of Lakṣmaṇa's arrows.

Rāma's centrality is even more marked in the RCM, where the respected elder Jāmbavān, instead of Hanumān, attempts to readjust Aṅgada's focus, which has become somewhat dimmed by depression. The four means are dropped altogether, and only the reminder discourse of the AdhyR (4:7:16-22) is preserved (RCM 4:26:6—4:do.26). While Vālmīki's Hanumān had to address, though in a manipulative way, the pivotal problem of the Aṅgada-Sugrīva relationship, the two other texts have chosen as if to disconnect the monkey king from his nephew's problem by having Āñjaneya and Jāmbavān redirect the latter's attention to Raghupati. This is not, however, only a matter of the Rāma figure's unfoldment, but also and consequently a question of the inappropriateness of any real suspicion between fellow *Rāmabhaktas*. Aṅgada's own increasingly minimal expressions of distrust of Sugrīva (AdhyR 4:7:4-6; RCM 4:26:3) are now regarded merely as the by-product spewing of a mind dejected at failure in the Lord's work and temporarily forgetful of His nature and its own purpose in the monkey incarnation.

For the AdhyR and the RCM's devotee Aṅgada, Hanumān's arguments are powerful and Jāmbavān's explanations, sublime. Consequently, he cannot but be convinced, and this conviction is in fact taken for granted, for rather than being explicitly mentioned, it is reflected in Aṅgada's subsequent behaviour (AdhyR 4:7:22; RCM 4:27:4). That is not the case, however, in the ValR. Rather than calming down and reassuring the distressed monkey, Āñjaneya seems to have added fuel to the fire, for Aṅgada begins to rail against Sugrīva more forcefully than ever (4:54:2-10), choosing death rather than return to Kiṣkindhā (4:54:11-12).

While Srinivas Sastri[6] considers this to be a failure in Hanumān's diplomacy, A. Wurm[7] believes the stress is rather on Aṅgada's "obliqueness" of mind and stubbornness, as well as the monkeys' fickleness. Though it is true that Māruti was unsuccessful, it is unlikely, given the circumstances, that anyone could have convinced Aṅgada, much less the engineer of the alliance which caused his father's death. The young monkey's condition, however, has very little to do with stubbornness, and much more with confusion in the face of a mass of hitherto suppressed thoughts and emotions. As for "obliqueness" of mind, it is far more applicable to power-craving, psychotic Sugrīva than to unfortunate Aṅgada, for the latter is a victim thereof, rather than a culprit therein.

As far as Hanumān is concerned, this scene shows his sense of loyalty to Sugrīva and responsibility to all the monkeys, which is interpreted, in the AdhyR, within a devotional framework. His inability, in the ValR, to convince Aṅgada only serves to underline his non-supernatural position in the *Kiṣkindhākāṇḍa*. And if it be questioned why the shrewdest of ministers even so much as attempted the task when he must surely have been aware of Aṅgada's justifiably unsympathetic feelings towards him and therefore the almost certain failure of his efforts, this may be explained simply by a lack of choice: Māruti had to do something, and within the perimeters of diplomacy, verbal convincing of Aṅgada was the only possible action which could have been beneficial to the *vānaras* as a whole, for, though the chance of bringing round Vālin's son was very slight, Hanumān could by his arguments persuade the monkeys, at least some of whom heard his speech, not to follow Aṅgada and thus minimize the problem.

REFERENCES

1. In the RCM, Aṅgada sees only death (4:26:2-3), and the monkeys then jointly decide that fasting unto death is preferable to returning without news of Sītā (4:26:5).
2. Though the *Tilaka* claims Aṅgada was too young to be able to protect the kingdom (KKlf, vol. 2, note on 4:22:5), it is to be noted that he was not too young to lead the southern expedition (4:40:5).
3. Not his sons, for he has none according to 4:53:21.
4. As he was dying, Vālin insisted not only on Sugrīva's rule (4:22:5), but also on Aṅgada's unconditional surrender to the latter's will (4:22:20,22), as well as, according to the *Amṛtakataka* and *Tilaka* (KKlf, vol.2, note on 4:22:14), the propriety of marital union between Sugrīva and Tārā.
5. Both in his last wishes (4:22:5,14,22) and in his apology to Rāma (4:18:42-44,57).
6. S.V.S. Sastri 1949, p. 264.
7. Wurm 1976, p. 152.

9

THE COAXING OF HANUMĀN

ValR 4:65-66
RCM 4:30:2-6

The old vulture Sampāti has seen Rāvaṇa carrying away Sītā (ValR 4:57:15-16)[1] and informs the monkeys of her whereabouts in the Aśoka grove (RCM 4:28:6) of the women's quarters (ValR 4:57:21) in the city of Laṅkā (ValR 4:57:20-21; RCM 4:28:6), well guarded by *rākṣasīs* (ValR 4:57:21). Now, however, they are faced with the dilemma of crossing the ocean. They vie with one another as to who can leap farther (ValR 4:64; RCM 4:29:3—4:30:1), each claiming a little more than the previous, yet not quite far enough.[2] While Jāmbavān explains that he is too old, Aṅgada believes he can only make a one-way trip, and besides, the bear objects to the latter's going, for Vālin's son is their leader. It may also be suggested that it would be rather absurd, as well as even further psychologically destabilizing and consequently a risk to the entire mission, for Vālmīki's Aṅgada to jeopardize his own life for the sake of the one who killed his father.[3]

In Tulasī's version, the story gains a further dimension, for Sampāti defines the qualifications of the one who can fulfil *Rāmakāja.* The source for this may be found in the AdhyR (4:8:55), which stipulates the prerequisite of faith. Tulasī (4:29:1-2) takes this instruction and expands it: the chosen monkey must have the physical strength to leap across the ocean (*jo nāghai sata jojana sāgara*), the courage (*taji kadarāī*) to face all obstacles, the intelligence (*mati āgara*) to outwit them, the firmness of mind (*mana dhīrā*) to endure all difficulties, and the presence of Rāma in his heart (*rāma hṛdayaṃ dharī*) so as to allow Him to do His own work.

Though the monkeys seem to have heard only the first qualification, for they boast solely of their strength,[4] it may be that they have registered everything, but fearing their own inability to deal with the *rākṣasas* and not wishing to admit it, they could be covering up their inadequacy by emphasizing what they do have, though in an insufficient quantity. Clear evidence for at least Jāmbavān's understanding of *all* of Sampāti's instructions is demonstrated in his later appraisal of Hanumān (4:30:2-3).[5]

While all of this is going on, Āñjaneya is silently sitting apart, not participating in the lively discussion (ValR 4:64:35; 4:65:2; RCM 4:30:2). His silence may be interpreted in a number of different ways: in the ValR he could be feeling somewhat insulted that Aṅgada has disregarded his advice and perhaps a little troubled at the latter's perception of him, for it is not unjustified;[6] based on the *Uttarakāṇḍa's* account of Āñjaneya's curse (7:36:28-33),[7] he may have forgotten his strength;[8] in the RCM, due to his absence of ego, he may see his might as coming from the Lord and thus cannot boast about what is not his own.[9]

Jāmbavān now steps in to persuade Hanumān that he is the only one equal to the task. The fact that no other monkey is capable of crossing the ocean has caused some difficulties for the ValR commentators because the *vānaras* in the other three expeditions easily crossed water to the ends of the earth. The *Tilaka* suggests that when the *rākṣasas* were building Laṅkā, they broke down and sank all intermediate mountains so that for the monkeys of the southern expedition there were no peaks left to touch down on every twenty to thirty *yojanas*.[10]

Jāmbavān's praise of Hanumān (ValR 4:65:2-7; RCM 4:30:2-3) may be understood as the stroking of a slightly wounded ego, the redirecting of a conscience-stricken mind from what cannot be changed to what can and must now be done, or the reminder either of his prowess or of his purpose for taking a monkey birth. In the ValR he emphasizes Āñjaneya's superior strength (*bala*), vigour (*tejas*), speed (*vega*), valour (*vikrama*), and intellect (*buddhi*), while in the RCM he points out that Hanumān has all the qualifications earlier enumerated by

Sampāti (4:29:1-2). The acclamation of his strength (*bala*), intellect (*buddhi*), discrimination (*viveka*), and wisdom (*vijñāna*), which correspond to all but the last of Sampāti's requirements,[11] have little effect on Tulasī's Māruti, for these do not belong to him, but to the Lord. It is the mention of the last requisite (the presence of Rāma in his heart), crystallized into the form of its consequence, Hanumān's incarnation for the sake of the Lord's work (*rāmakāja lagi tava avatāra*), that finally spurs him to action, for he is love of Rāma in bodily manifestation, *Rāmabhakti* in solidified shape. Vālmīki's Hanumān, however, needs more convincing, and therefore Jāmbavān recounts Āñjaneya's birth and youthful exploits (4:65:8-27).

This portion of Jāmbavān's coaxing introduces Hanumān's extraordinary aspect, as opposed to the ordinary, though ideal, *saciva*. From now on, he is portrayed with supernatural dimensions, hair-raising abilities, and mind-blowing feats.

The ValR gives two accounts of Hanumān's origin and early years,[12] the second (7:35-36) being more detailed than the first (4:65:8-27). He is born from monkey Āñjanā, the wife of Kesarin, and Vāyu (4:65:8-18; 7:35:19-20).[13] In his childhood, hunger prompts him to leap at the sun, for he thinks it to be a fruit (4:65:19; 7:35:23). Rāhu, whose time it is to consume Sūrya, complains to Indra (7:35:31-45), who then strikes Hanumān with his thunderbolt. The youngster falls to the ground, and due to his broken left jaw (*hanu*), acquires the name "Hanumān" (4:65:21-22; 7:35:47; 7:36:11).[14] Angry Vāyu stops blowing and all beings suffer (4:65:23-24; 7:35:48-51). He resumes his function only when Prajāpati has restored Hanumān to life (7:36:3). The gods then bestow boons on Āñjaneya, who will carry out all that they have to accomplish (7:36:9): Indra makes him invulnerable to the thunderbolt (7:36:12) and gives him choice as to his own death (4:65:27); Sūrya provides him with one hundredth part of his effulgence, and eloquence when learning the *Śāstras* (7:36:13-14); Varuṇa promises that for innumerable years his noose and waters will not kill him (7:36:15); Yama blesses him with absence of disease, unassailableness, and freedom from dejection in battle (7:36:16); Kubera's[15] mace will not defeat him when fighting (7:36:17); Śiva's shafts will not wound him (7:36:18); Brahmā's instruments of combat will not harm him (4:65:25; 7:36:19); and he will be invulnerable to the divine weapons created by Viśvakarman (7:36:20-21). Brahmā then concludes that Māruti will be the terror of his foes, the support of his friends, and, invincible, he will perform hair-raising feats for the destruction of Rāvaṇa and the gratification of Rāma (7:36:23-24).

Proud of all his boons, Hanumān disturbs the sacrifices of the *ṛṣis*, who eventually curse him to forget his power for a long time (7:36:28-33). Later passages add that he will remember it in the pursuit of a friend's purpose,[16] and his strength will increase.[17] Therefore, Jāmbavān provides the reminder which finally convinces Āñjaneya to leap across the ocean.

In comparing the various means employed by Jāmbavān to coax Hanumān in the different texts, the AdhyR provides the connecting link. While Vālmīki gives a detailed account of Āñjaneya's youthful adventures, the AdhyR (4:9:19) briefly mentions his leap at the sun, which Tulasī Dāsa omits altogether. The AdhyR (4:9:18) adds the purpose of his birth (*Rāmakārya*), making it the central argument, and this is duplicated, in Tulasī's own fashion, in the RCM. Hanumān's own early experiences, since they do not include Rāma, lose importance for Tulasī Dāsa, and even the characteristics of Āñjaneya that are preserved from the ValR are now transferred to Raghupati: Māruti's strength becomes the Lord's strength.

Jāmbavān's coaxing of Hanumān awakens the latter's dormant extraordinary potential. Filled with power, he grows to an unsurpassed form (ValR 4:66:2) the size of a mountain (RCM 4:30:3), his body shining like gold (RCM 4:30:4),[18] his mouth blazing like the sun and glowing like smokeless fire (ValR 4:66:4), and he begins to roar like a lion (RCM 4:30:4).

Vālmīki's Hanumān is overtaken with the same pride that led to his curse, and he begins to boast (4:66:6-25) of his parentage with Vāyu (4:66:7), of his unequalled leaping

(4:66:7), likening himself to lightning (4:66:21), Mount Meru (4:66:18), Garuḍa (4:66:20), Vāyu (4:66:24), and Viṣṇu (4:66:22),[19] claiming that he can circle thousands of times around Garuḍa (4:66:11) or Meru (4:66:8), meet the sun (4:66:12),[20] go ten thousand *yojanas* (4:66:24), steal nectar from the hands of Indra or Brahmā (4:66:25)... in brief, there is none greater than him. In his might he can make mountains tremble (4:66:15,19),[21] flowers will follow him as he leaps (4:66:16),[22] he can tear up (4:66:14) or flood (4:66:9) the earth, stir up the ocean (4:66:9,14,19), and even lift up Laṅkā[23] and carry it away (4:66:25). "I will find Sītā",[24] he roars.

Tulasī's Hanumān, though humble by nature, does give in to excitement and claims he can easily cross the ocean, kill Rāvaṇa and his army, uproot Mount Trikuṭa and bring it back (RCM 4:30:4-5).[25] His pride, however, is only excessive enthusiasm and energy at the opportunity to fulfil *Rāmakāja*, for he is not essentially boastful. Therefore, as soon as he has said this, he catches himself, realizing he has overstepped the limit, and humbly requests the elder Jāmbavān's advice—behaviour which would be inconceivable for Vālmīki's Hanumān at this high, high point.

Thus, in the RCM, following the AdhyR (4:9:26), Jāmbavān brings Āñjaneya down a little bit, balancing him out by telling him that his only task is to see Sītā and bring back news from her. Rāma will then do the rest (4:30:6).[26] To have Hanumān do more would be inappropriate, for it would not be based on Rāma's wishes, and it would render the Lord's birth futile, apart from the fact that it would prevent so many *rākṣasas* from attaining liberation by dying at His hands.

As for Vālmīki's Jāmbavān, he has no objection to Hanumān's boasting, for the monkeys are only too happy finally to see that the work will be done and their lives will be spared. They vow to stand on one foot until he returns (4:66:30), while in the RCM (5:1:1), Māruti orders them to live on fruits, roots, and bulbs.

As he prepares to go, Vālmīki's Āñjaneya is full of pride, but Tulasī's Māruti is abounding in humility. Both are certain of the favourable outcome, one due to confidence in himself, the other, following the AdhyR (5:1:2), due to faith in and surrender to Rāma.

REFERENCES

1. The ValR has two versions of the story, the first (4:57) less detailed than the second (4:58). In the latter, it is Sampāti's son Supārśva who sees Rāvaṇa abducting Sītā (4:58:15-23).
2. The *Rāmāyaṇaśiromaṇi* claims that the denigrations of their respective leaping powers are merely to encourage Hanumān to display his own prowess (KKlf, vol. 2, note on 4:65:33).
3. The ValR passage (4:57:8-10) wherein Aṅgada takes an active role in questioning Sampāti as to Rāvaṇa's hiding place may be interpreted either as a return to his earlier state of repression or, quite possibly, as a slightly later layer of the ValR.
4. Based on RCM lectures by Swami Tejomayananda.
5. See pp. 60-61.
6. Maheśvaratīrtha, based on 4:64:35 wherein Hanumān is said to be seated at ease (*sukhopaviṣṭa*), does not consider him to be dejected in any way, but rather confident of his ability to accomplish "easily" this task which no one else can do (KKlf, vol. 2, note on 4:64:35). This view is not mentioned in the above list of interpretations, for it explains his ease rather than his silence.
7. See p. 62.
8. This is also the reason given for the fact that Hanumān, though of greater strength than even Vālin and Rāvaṇa (ValR 7:35:2), did not destroy Vālin for the protection of Sugrīva (ValR 7:35:11-16).
9. Based on RCM lectures by Swami Tejomayananda.
10. KKlf, vol. 2, note on 4:65:36.
11. *bala*: *jo nāghai sata jojana sāgara; buddhi*: *mati āgara*; *viveka, vijñāna*: *taji kadarāī, mana dhīrā.* (One with discrimination and wisdom sees that there is nothing to fear and can therefore hold firm in the face of difficulties, wisely exercising strength and patience. *Taji kadarāī* and *mana dhīrā* are the effects directly dependent on *viveka* and *vijñāna.*)
12. According to Lefeber (KKlf, vol. 2, note on 4:65:18), the first account of his childhood (4:65:19-27ab) is a later interpolation because the story flows smoothly without it, and it is retold in greater detail in 7:35:13—7:36:26.
13. For varying accounts of Hanumān's birth and youth as presented in the *Rāmāyaṇas* and the *Purāṇas*, see Mani 1975, pp. 307-308.
14. Literally, "Hanumān" means "having a jaw". Lefeber notes that the sense is that of a large jaw, as monkeys have, rather than a broken one, as the story implies (KKlf, vol. 2, note on 4:65:22).

15. *Ekākṣipiṅgala* is, according to the *Vivekatilaka* (in crit. ed. footnotes), Vaiśravaṇa (Kubera).
16. Crit. ed., passage 723 inserted following 7:36:33.
17. Crit. ed., passage 724 inserted following 7:36:33.
18. Cf. RCM 5:ś1.3 : *hemaśailābhadehaṃ.*
19. Jāmbavān has already likened him to Viṣṇu in 4:65:35.
20. Cf. 7:36:42. Hanumān learned grammar from Sūrya by travelling with him through the sky.
21. This is actualized in 5:1:11.
22. This is actualized in 5:1:50.
23. Cf. 5:1:39.
24. *ahaṃ drakṣyāmi vaidehīṃ* (4:66:23). Cf. 5:1:39.
25. Vālmīki gives a similar statement just before Hanumān leaps (5:1:36-39), as does the AdhyR (4:9:22-23).
26. In the AdhyR (4:9:26), Jāmbavān also tells Hanumān that the latter may then return to Laṅkā with Rāma, at which time only he may show his manliness (*pauruṣa*), as opposed to the well-intentioned, though boastful, monkeyness (*kapitva*) he has just exhibited.

10

THE LEAP ACROSS THE OCEAN

ValR 4:66—5:1
RCM 5:1:3—5:3:3

The Lift-off

ValR 4:66:31—5:1:75
RCM 5:1:3-4

As he prepares to jump, Vālmīki's Hanumān continues his boastful assertions, announcing for all to hear that the mere earth cannot hold him and that therefore he must resort to Mount Mahendra (4:66:31-32). The truth is that it is simply easier to fly from a mountain. In the RCM (5:1:3), humbler than a blade of grass, Āñjaneya does not ostensibly point out anyone's inability to bear his weight, but for practical purposes, he intelligently spots a mountain and playfully springs on top of it. His light and playful (*kautuka*) manner expresses both ease and humility: he does not land in a loud, boisterous, attention-craving way, but rather joyfully, gently, and effortlessly. Tulasī Dāsa's monkey has lost much of his *kapitva*, and his refined and profoundly self-effacing behaviour has gained him glory in all the three worlds.

Though Mahendra is unharmed by the landing of the RCM's Māruti, it suffers considerably in the ValR (4:66:38-43): crushed by Hanumān's feet, the mountain cries out (4:66:38) and despairs (4:66:43), as its rocks and trees shoot forth, as its waters are released (4:66:39), as all beings, including animals and seers, either abandon it in fear or hide (4:66:40-43). Again, when Āñjaneya is preparing to leap up, Vālmīki describes Mahendra's lot in quite some detail (5:1:11-28). As Hanumān had boasted earlier (4:66:15-16,19), the mountain shakes, flowers fall (5:1:11), even more water shoots forth (5:1:13), and this time minerals are released (5:1:14). Snakes emerge (5:1:17), cave-dwellers roar (5:1:15), ascetics think Mahendra is being shattered by the elements (*bhūtas*),[1] whilst the seers (*ṛṣis*), celestial bards (*cāraṇas*), and perfected beings (*siddhas*) alone know that Hanumān is about to leap across the ocean for the sake of Rāma and the monkeys (5:1:26-28). This last statement, of course, calls back to mind Āñjaneya's earlier attitude to Rāma and the responsibility he feels to protect the monkeys. Fear is the moving force.

Tulasī, on the other hand, merely mentions that when Hanumān finally leaps up towards Laṅkā, the mountain sinks down to the nether world (Pātāla).[2] Though this decreases the account of Mahendra's plight from a detailed description to a very brief mention, it nonetheless magnifies Māruti's might. Tulasī's Āñjaneya is far humbler and proportionally more powerful because it is not his might, but Rāma's. The more he lets go of his ego, the more perfect a vehicle he becomes for Raghupati to work through; and since the Lord is infinitely powerful, Hanumān becomes all-powerful. It may be true that Tulasī lacks Vālmīki's beautiful description, but that is not his purpose, for he only desires to glorify Rāma and the *Rāmabhaktas* who by their very being express that glorification of the Lord and whose beauty lies in bringing forth Rāma's beauty.

As far as Hanumān's mental preparation is concerned, Vālmīki describes him as concentrating his mind on Laṅkā (4:66:44), thereby fully focusing on his goal by bringing all his energy to bear in that direction, and then saluting Sūrya, Indra, Vāyu, Brahmā, and all beings (5:1:7-8), to which some MSS[3] add Śiva, Skanda, Yama, Varuṇa, Rāma, Lakṣmaṇa, Sītā, Sugrīva, the *ṛṣis*, the forefathers (*pitṛs*), and Kubera—obviously later material reflecting Māruti's change of attitude towards Rāma due to the unfoldment of the latter's image. Having zeroed in on his destination and asked blessings of the gods, he makes the intention to go (5:1:7). Tulasī Dāsa does not really see the need for focusing on the work itself, but converges rather on the One for Whom the work is being done: Rāma is to be invoked again and again (5:1:3), and He will thereby take care of all concentration. In fact, He alone will Himself do the work if the vehicle is properly tuned up to

Him, in which case there can be no failures, mistakes, or setbacks, nor is there cause to fear on the part of the *bhakta*. As expressed in the *Nārada Bhakti Sūtra* (61), "No worry or anxiety should be entertained at the worldly losses, since [it is the nature of the true devotee constantly] to surrender [his limited] self and [all its] secular and sacred activities [to the Lord of his heart]."[4]

The relevance of "again and again" (*bāra bāra*) is that the *bhakta* does not just call on the Lord and then jump into his work, forgetting all about Him, nor is his invocation merely a formality, but rather a full, unending, whole-hearted form of worship that goes on from the beginning of the task to the end. If at any point Hanumān were to lose track of Rāma, *he* would be the one acting, and not Rāma acting *through him*. This might lead not only to possible imperfections in the work, but, much more seriously, to the interference in and the obstruction of Raghupati's work. *Rāmakāja* implies that Rāma Himself fulfils His own purpose.[5] Therefore, if Hanumān is found to be "doing" anything, then it is not *Rāmakāja* that he does.

The shift in Rāma's position and the consequent re-definition of the other characters' relationships to him may be clearly traced in the invocations of the different texts. The earlier layer of the ValR could not present Hanumān saluting the Rāghava, for the latter was neither a god nor God Himself, and Āñjaneya distrusted him. There is, therefore, a formal entreating of the *devas,* to which, in a later layer of the ValR, Rāma is added, and finally, as he is recognized as an incarnation of Viṣṇu, He is called upon unceasingly in the RCM. Hanumān thus moves from a self-reliant character to a Rāma-reliant one. This change in his position will become increasingly evident in the *Sundarakāṇḍa,* as he is found to go far above and beyond the call of duty to fulfil the alliance, which is slowly becoming the service of Viṣṇu's *avatāra.*

As concerns Āñjaneya's physical preparation, Tulasī omits it, for, as has been seen, all that is necessary is to be attuned to Rāma, Who does everything. Vālmīki, however, provides a detailed description (5:1:9-35): swelling his body (5:1:9),[6] Hanumān presses Mahendra with his feet and arms (5:1:10), shakes his bodily hairs, roars loudly (5:1:29), whirls his tail (5:1:30), his arms become as iron clubs, he contracts his waist and sinks down (5:1:32), draws in his arms and neck (5:1:33), flattens his ears (5:1:35), and filled with *vīrya* and *tejas* (5:1:33), a state of concentrated power and energy focused in the lower part of his body, he scans the sky in order to see a clear path for himself, having arrested his vital air (*prāṇa*) in his heart (5:1:34).[7] Strangely enough, after such a buildup of extensive and intense preparation, he now says a few words to the monkeys (5:1:35). (Under normal circumstances all previous effort would be lost.) He proclaims his intention to go to Laṅkā and find Sītā, wherever she may be, or to uproot Rāvaṇa's city and bring it back (5:1:36-39). One would think that before taking his leap, he would once again have to undergo the above physical preparations, at the very least the focusing of his energy and the holding of his *prāṇa* in the heart, but not so, for Hanumān simply leaps.

While Tulasī Dāsa omits a description of the lift-off, Vālmīki indulges in it. The speed with which Hanumān rises causes trees to be sucked up (5:1:41). As he himself had predicted and bragged about (4:66:16), flowers follow him in his flight (5:1:50). In fact, even clouds are directly behind him (5:1:70). Just as he had threatened and boasted of his ability to swallow the sky (4:66:18), he appears here as if he were about to drink up the ocean and suck up the firmament (5:1:53). His eyes are like lightning (5:1:54) and like sun and moon (5:1:55), as his form of ten *yojanas* in width and thirty in length (5:1:69) covers the sky. His tail is likened to Indra's banner (5:1:57), and he himself is like Garuḍa (5:1:68). Though only leaping, he resembles the king of the birds in full flight— an ability no doubt connected to his parentage with Vāyu. The latter also serves him, presumably as a cool breeze, just as Sūrya, his preceptor in grammar (7:36:42), spares him from heat (5:1:72).[8]

While Vālmīki states that Hanumān leaped up with "speed" (*vega*),[9] Tulasī characterizes the lift-off with the word "might" (*bala*).[10] Speed connotes the efficiency of the ideal *saciva*, whereas might expresses power and greatness, which, in Tulasī's context, are not so much Āñjaneya's as they are

Rāma's. It may be noted that *bala* is the first quality that is described in the RCM's invocation (5:śl.3) of Hanumān. He is *atulitabaladhāma*, "the abode of immeasurable or unequalled strength", for he is the container of Raghupati's infinite strength. In the *Bhagavad Gītā* (7:11) it is said that "I am the strength of the strong",[11] but *bala* is defined as being "devoid of desire and attachment".[12] In remaining ever in a state of total surrender to the Lord, Hanumān begins his task with Rāma's *bala* and proceeds therein like the unerring shaft (*amogha bānā*) of Raghupati (RCM 5:1:4).[13] The shaft (Māruti) is undeluded and therefore unerring, precisely because it is propelled by Rāma, Who is omniscient. Also, since His arrows always return to His quiver (e.g. 6:do.13b), Hanumān's success is assured.

The Obstacles

ValR 5:1:75-180
RCM 5:1:5—5:3:3

As Āñjaneya leaps across the ocean, he encounters three obstacles: Mount Maināka, Surasā, and Siṃhikā. Though the first of these is by no means intended to obstruct him, because it slows him down, it may be considered to stand between him and his work.

Maināka

ValR 5:1:75-122
RCM 5:1:5—5:do.1

When Sāgara (the Ocean) sees Hanumān coursing along, he calls on Mount Maināka to rise from the depths of the ocean and offer him rest (ValR 5:1:75-88; RCM 5:1:5). While in the ValR the motive for aiding Rāma's *dūta* is the return of favours from a member of the Ikṣvāku race, to which the Rāghavas also belong (5:1:77), and from Vāyu (5:1:108-13);[14] in the RCM it is out of love for Raghupati (5:1:5). In both texts, Hanumān is being offered aid, not because of his identity, but due to his function. Vālmīki honours him because of the parentage of the one whose envoy he happens to be, whereas in the RCM it is due to Āñjaneya's own personal connection with the Lord. As a vehicle of Rāma, he is Rāma in different form, and therefore, in seeing him, Sāgara and Maināka see the Lord.[15]

Upon catching sight of the mountain, Vālmīki's Hanumān assumes it is an obstacle (5:1:94) and pushes it aside with his chest (5:1:95). Maināka then takes a human form, and standing on its own peak (5:1:97), offers him rest and food (5:1:98, 102), and explains Sāgara's (5:1:99) and its own (5:1:108-113) purpose for extending him hospitality.[16] In the AdhyR and the RCM, however, Āñjaneya, as the Omniscient's messenger and vehicle, knows full well that this is no intended obstruction, though the AdhyR (5:1:30-32) maintains Maināka's introduction.[17] Tulasī's omission of the mountain's speech reflects his total absorption in Raghupati, for since the personal relationship between Hanumān and Maināka is based on a connection with Vāyu[18] rather than Rāma, it is of secondary importance.

Āñjaneya refuses to rest until the Rāghava's work is done, and therefore touches the mountain with his hand and flies on (ValR 5:1:117-18; RCM 5:do.1). This may be understood as the ideal *dūta* at work, and perhaps in a hurry due to some lingering (though gradually fading) doubts about Rāma, or as the ideal *bhakta* in his unerring flight to Sītā and then back to Raghupati.

Vālmīki (5:1:122) makes his own assessment of Hanumān's action by asserting that this is the second difficult feat which he has succeeded in accomplishing, the first being the leaping up to get across the ocean. Vālmīki obviously wants to underline the greatness of Hanumān's feats.

Surasā

ValR 5:1:130-56
RCM 5:2:1—5:do.2

The Surasā episode, according to J.C. Jhala,[19] is a duplication, both in conception and details of description, of the Siṃhikā obstacle.[20] Further evidence for its later interpolation is its absence from the Mbh and *Agni Purāṇa* accounts of the *Rāmakathā*.

In an attempt to test Hanumān, the *devas, gandharvas,*[21] *siddhas,* and *ṛṣis* send Surasā, the mother of the serpents (*nāgas*), to obstruct him (ValR 5:1:130-33; RCM 5:2:1). The question arises, however, as to why the gods would want to place an obstacle before their own messenger, who is about to do their work (ValR 7:36:9). At least four explanations may be given: they doubt Hanumān's abilities; they have confidence in him, but desire to sharpen their instrument; out of concern for him, they may wish to give him advance warning of the nature of the coming obstacles; or this may be a means to reveal Hanumān's greatness and thereby demonstrate that he truly is perfect for the task. For Tulasī, the last reason is the only possibility, for to test or even to doubt the ideal *bhakta* is to doubt and test the Lord. While the AdhyR (5:1:9-10) seems to favour the first option, Vālmīki may have any or all of the above in mind.

In the ValR (5:1:133), the *devas* want to know the extent of Hanumān's strength and heroism; whereas in the RCM (5:2:1), following the AdhyR (5:1:12), they are interested in his strength and intellect—the two first qualifications enumerated by Sampāti (4:29:1), which Jāmbavān had stated earlier that Āñjaneya has in all fullness (4:30:2). It is also to be noted that *bala* comes before *buddhi,* for *bala* (*Rāmabala*), as noted earlier, is Hanumān's highly prominent characteristic in the RCM.[22] As for the third of Sampāti's qualifications, *bhakti,* it has already been demonstrated in Hanumān's leaping up and his willingness to meet the challenge.

Surasā approaches her victim, loudly announcing that the gods have provided her with food in the form of Āñjaneya (ValR 5:1:136; AdhyR 5:1:14; RCM 5:2:2), and even going so far as to demand that he enter her mouth (ValR 5:1:136; AdhyR 5:1:13). Clearly, she is issuing a challenge rather than intending solely to eat him, for she would not otherwise take the chance of losing her prey by giving it warning of her incoming attack.[23] In this light, her statement may be reexamined for possible clues as to her purpose: though in other circumstances it would be considered as incidental, here, her immediate reference to the gods may be interpreted as pointing to those whose mission this properly is and whose messenger she merely happens to be. Perceptive Hanumān is no doubt aware of the less than straightforward nature of this obstacle, and he does not, therefore, just brush it aside in one quick stroke. His initial response is conciliatory (*sāma* and *dāna*): he explains the task he is currently engaged in and requests the permission first to complete it, promising then to return (ValR 5:1:138-41; RCM 5:2:2-3). In the AdhyR (5:1:14) and the RCM (5:2:3), he is most respectful to her, addressing her as "mother". When that approach fails (ValR 5:1:142; RCM 5:2:3), he resorts to *bheda*, angrily provoking her to open her mouth (ValR 5:1:143; AdhyR 5:1:17) and challenging her to eat him (RCM 5:2:3)— follow-ups directly parallel to Surasā's first statements. This tactic ultimately leads to *daṇḍa* in the form of a contest between Surasā's ability to increase the size of her mouth and Āñjaneya's capacity to grow larger. Each in turn outdo one another until she has extended her mouth to one hundred *yojanas* (ValR 5:1:144-49; RCM 5:2:4-5). Intelligent Hanumān now shrinks to the size of a thumb (*aṅguṣṭhamātraka*),[24] enters her mouth, and immediately comes out (ValR 5:1:152; RCM 5:2:6), thereby conquering through his *buddhi* and symbolically through humility. He salutes her (ValR 5:1:153; RCM 5:2:6), and in the ValR, is immediately on his way (5:1:153), hardly waiting to hear her blessing (5:1:155). In the RCM, however, Āñjaneya's awareness of the inordinate nature of this obstacle, already confirmed by the fact that she is the only one of the intended obstructions whom he does not physically abuse, is further emphasized as he begs leave of her (5:1:6), awaiting her last word. She now openly reveals her mission for the *devas* and states that she has accomplished her task; that is, to find out the secret (*maramu*) of his *buddhi* and *bala* (RCM 5:2:6). The change of word order from the *bala* and *buddhi* (RCM 5:2:1), which the gods wanted to test, to the *buddhi* and *bala* (RCM 5:2:6), that she has discovered, is significant. It is primarily Hanumān's *buddhi*, as indicated by the AdhyR's Surasā when she addresses him as the foremost amongst the intelligent (*buddhimatāṃ vara*),[25] rather than, but also in addition to, his *bala*, which allowed him to overcome the obstacle. Therefore, in this particular circumstance, it is *buddhi* over *bala*, as opposed to the usual precedence of *bala* (RCM 5:do.2).

While Vālmīki's Surasā wishes Āñjaneya success (5:1:155), the RCM (5:do.2), following the AdhyR (5:1:24), predicts it with certainty and in all its fullness.[26] And once again, the ValR (5:1:156) underlines this as the third difficult feat accomplished by Hanumān.

Siṃhikā

ValR 5:1:166-80
RCM 5:3:1-3

Siṃhikā is a marine demoness who feeds on birds flying in the sky by catching hold of their shadows and thus trapping them through her *māyā* (RCM 5:3:1). Sugrīva referred to her when he was dispatching the southern expedition (ValR 4:40:26). When she grasps Hanumān's shadow, Vālmīki's Āñjaneya remembers this warning and recognizes her (5:1:171), whereas in the RCM he is left to himself to ascertain the situation. While Tulasī merely mentions that Hanumān kills her (5:3:3), Vālmīki gives a longer description (5:1:172-77) resembling the Surasā episode: Māruti increases his size, while she, in response, stretches her mouth wide open as if from the nether world to the sky, after which he contracts his body, enters her mouth, and tears up her insides, quickly flying out again. And this, Vālmīki describes as a terrifying (*bhīma)* action (5:1:179).

These three obstacles are practical demonstrations of Hanumān's physical strength, intelligence, alertness, endurance, and loyalty to Sugrīva, the monkeys, and Rāma, as well as his gradually increasing *Rāmabhakti*. Though the positions in the ValR and the RCM vary, the former is clearly beginning to move closer to the latter.

Eventually, Hanumān begins to approach Laṅkā (ValR 5:1:182), and considering that his giant body will attract attention (ValR 5:1:186), he assumes his own natural form (ValR 5:1:187), which has the added quality of being invincible (*aśakyapratipannarūpa)*.[27] Finally, he reaches Mount Trikuṭa (ValR 5:1:189; RCM 5:3:3).

REFERENCES

1. 5:1:20.
2. 5:1:4.
3. Crit. ed., passage 8 inserted following 5:1:7ab.
4. *lokahānau cintā na kāryā niveditātmalokavedaśīlatvāt* // Translation by Swami Chinmayananda in *Nārada Bhakti Sūtra* 1982.
5. See pp. 48-49.
6. Cf. 4:65:36; 4:66:1.
7. In the Mbh (3:266:58), Hanumān enters Vāyu.
8. This passage (5:1:72) may not necessarily be familiar with 7:36:42, but for later generations the connection is obvious.
   In the Mbh (3:148-50), Bhīma, who is also the son of Vāyu, encounters the aged Hanumān (for it is now a new *yuga*) and asks to see the form the latter took when leaping across the ocean. Āñjaneya refuses due to his old age, but Bhīma insists. Therefore, though he can grow much larger, Āñjaneya shows him only so much as the latter can bear to see. Bhīma, like Arjuna at the sight of Kṛṣṇa's cosmic manifestation in the *Bhagavad Gītā* (11:45), is terrified at the horrific yet resplendent form and asks Hanumān to contract himself.
9. 5:1:40.
10. 5:1:3.
11. *balaṃ balavatām asmi.*
12. *kāmarāgavivarjitam.*
13. Vālmīki (5:1:36) also makes this comparison, as does the AdhyR (5:1:3). Clearly, the unfoldment of the Rāma figure is in progress, but the full meaning of the simile does not reach its culmination until placed in the hands of Tulasī Dāsa.
14. See note 16 below.
15. This phenomenon is demonstrated when Vibhīṣaṇa mistakes Hanumān for Raghupati (RCM 5:6:4) and when Bharata says to Āñjaneya: "Today I have met in you my beloved Rāma." (RCM 7:2:6).
16. The Ocean had been increased by Sagara of the Ikṣvāku race, an ancestor of Rāma's, and consequently wishes to help the Rāghava's messenger (5:1:77). As for Maināka, his devotion is to Hanumān's father: in the Kṛta *yuga*, when mountains had wings and would fly about everywhere, all beings were afraid that the flying masses might fall down, and therefore Indra cut off their wings, but he missed Maināka's, for Vāyu carried the latter away, dropping him safely into the ocean (5:1:108-13).

17. Note that in the AdhyR, the Maināka episode follows the Surasā obstruction.
18. See note 16 above.
19. Crit. ed., *Sundarakāṇḍa,* pp. xxxii-xxxiii.
20. The Siṃhikā episode is discussed on p. 75.
21. Celestial musicians.
22. See p. 71.
23. Based on RCM lectures by Swami Tejomayananda.
24. ValR 5:1:151. The RCM (5:2:5) is less specific, mentioning only a very small form (*ati laghu rūpa).*
25. 5:1:23.
26. Not just *rāma kāju,* but *rāma kāju sabu.*
27. ValR 5:1:188.

11

THE SEARCH FOR SĪTĀ

ValR 5:2-13
RCM 5:3:3—5:do.8

The Entry into Laṅkā

ValR 5:2-3
RCM 5:3:3—5:5:2

As he observes the well-fortified city (ValR 5:2:14-16,21-22; RCM 5:3:5), Vālmīki's Āñjaneya is filled with mental agitation (*kapitva)*, for he fears that even the *devas* and Rāma would be unable to enter it, much less the monkeys, who could not even cross the ocean (5:2:25-26). He collects himself and determines to find out whether Sītā is still alive (5:2:29).

Tulasī Dāsa omits this, as well as every other fit of *kapitva* that arises in the ValR, for the ideal *bhakta* has no cause to worry. So long as Māruti remains the perfect instrument, he need not even think about what he should or should not do, as his actions are spontaneous expressions of Rāma's will. The direct and instantaneous translation of the heart's (Raghupati's abode) command into action renders decision-making unnecessary, and in fact, obstructive to the divine process.

Vālmīki's Hanumān now turns his thoughts to the means of entering Laṅkā. Clearly, it must be at night, and his form must be invisible (*lakṣyālakṣya rūpa*).[1] Again his mind reaches a state of *kapitva*, and rather than concentrating on what form he should assume, he worries about spoiling the entire enterprise and about the difficulty of meeting Sītā privately (5:2:36). He then begins to reason as to how, in general, success is attained and what the obstacles to it are: success is based on right time (*kāla*) and right place (*deśa*), and if these two conditions are not fulfilled, failure is certain (5:2:37).

Furthermore, an emissary must not be conceited (*paṇḍitamānin*), for that is yet another cause for failure (5:2:38).[2] Having set down the basic principles and pitfalls in performing a duty, Hanumān reverts to his own predicament, though representing his doubts in a general manner: how can the task at hand be unfoiled, and how can confusion be avoided (5:2:39)? Again he turns back to the problem of being unseen by the *rākṣasas*. He fully realizes that if he is spotted, Rāma's efforts to destroy Rāvaṇa will be without success (5:2:40). What will then happen to all the monkeys and especially to Sugrīva? Āñjaneya feels the responsibility weighing on his shoulders. Now that he has reached Laṅkā, how horrible it would be if he failed. Fear sets in as he worries that the *rākṣasas* will recognize him even if he takes a *rākṣasa* form (5:2:41). The city is so well protected that even Vāyu, his own father, subtle and invisible as he is, would be unable to go unnoticed (5:2:42). So what now? If he keeps his own form, he will certainly be caught and killed (5:2:43). Therefore, he must take a small (*hrasva*) form (5:2:44).

The AdhyR and the RCM omit all mental discoursing, for Hanumān is completely calm and self-controlled. His reasoning is brief, direct, and clear: at the sight of the guards, he concludes that in order not to be seen, he must assume a very minute form (*ati laghu rūpa*)[3] and enter Laṅkā by night (AdhyR 5:1:42; RCM 5:do.3). Nothing more and nothing less.

Vālmīki's Hanumān takes a figure the size of a cat (*pṛṣadaṃśakamātra*),[4] whereas in the AdhyR (5:3:20) it is the size of a bird (*kalaviṅkapramāṇa*), and in the RCM (5:4:1), that of a mosquito (*masaka samāna*). Obviously, Āñjaneya is gradually being given greater power, for the smaller the form, the more places it can enter and the lesser the likelihood of its being noticed.

While in the critical edition of the ValR, Māruti simply jumps unto the city walls (5:3:7), and following some observations, enters Laṅkā (5:3:20), in the northern recension,[5] the AdhyR (5:1:43-57), and the RCM (5:4:1—5:5:2), he is prevented from doing so by the demoness Laṅkinī. This would be the fourth obstacle, which, by its presence, enhances

Hanumān's status due to his ability to overcome yet another difficulty. She does not, however, keep him for long, as he deals her a terrible blow with his fist, and she falls down vomiting blood (AdhyR 5:1:46; RCM 5:4:2). Rather than being upset, she is delighted and feels blessed to have met Rāma's *dūta.* Much earlier, she had received a clue from Brahmā as to the time of destruction of the demon race: the dreaded moment was to be at hand when a monkey would punch her (AdhyR 5:1:48-53; RCM 5:4:3-4).[6] She blesses Hanumān, telling him to enter Laṅkā with Rāma in his heart and accomplish his (His) work (RCM 5:5:1). She leaves no doubt as to his success when she states that all is possible and in fact easy for him on whom Rāma has cast His glance (RCM 5:5:1-2): poison becomes nectar, enemies become friends (as in her own case), the ocean shrinks to the size of a cow's footprint[7] (as in the crossing of the ocean), fire becomes cool (as will be seen in the burning of Laṅkā), and Mount Meru appears like a grain of sand (as will be demonstrated when he will be carrying the Himalayan peak to the battle site).[8] In the AdhyR (5:1:54-56) she even informs him of Sītā's exact whereabouts. This honour, in the RCM, is reserved for devotee Vibhīṣaṇa (5:8:3).

Therefore, apart from glorifying Hanumān and thereby Rāma, this fourth obstacle foreshadows the destruction of the *rākṣasas,* thus assuring the successful outcome of Āñjaneya's mission, and Rāma's ultimate victory. It may also be noted that the three *intended* obstructions counterbalance one another: Surasā attacks from the sky (space), Siṃhikā from the ocean (water), and Laṅkinī from the earth,[9] thus representing three of the five elements.

In the RCM (5:5:2), Hanumān then enters Laṅkā, holding Rāma in his heart. In the ValR, however, as he stands on the city wall observing the fortress (5:3:7-12), once again he is filled with doubts and fear. For a while he thinks it is not possible for anyone to invade Laṅkā (5:3:14), and upon regaining control of himself by concentrating on Rāma's and Lakṣmaṇa's heroism (5:3:17),[10] he finally enters the city (5:3:20).

The Search through Laṅkā

ValR 5:3-12
RCM 5:5:3—5:8:3

Vālmīki gives a very detailed description of the search through Laṅkā, expressing Hanumān's wonder and delight at the splendour of the city and the life of its people (5:4-9)—no doubt an audience-captivator.[11] E.B. Cowell in his introduction to the *Buddhacarita*[12] has noted the similarity of the epic's "nightly seraglio scene"[13] (ValR 5:7-9) to a portion of Aśvaghoṣa's work (5:47ff.). The fact that this section is essential to the latter text, for "it supplies the final impulse which stirs the Bodhisattva [the Buddha] to make his escape from the world",[14] and that it is merely ornamental in the ValR, points to an imitation on the part of a later interpolator of the ValR.

The AdhyR (5:2:1), on the other hand, merely mentions that Laṅkā is most beautiful (*paramaśobhanā*), while Tulasī Dāsa (5:3:ch.1-3) depicts, in a considerably shorter form than the ValR,[15] the city and its activities. Due to the impurity of the *rākṣasas*, he would be inclined to follow the AdhyR in omitting any description whatsoever, but he finds it necessary, for the demons "will drop their bodies at the *tīrtha*[16] of Rāma's arrows"[17] and thus attain salvation (5:3:ch.3).

Hanumān searches through all parts of Laṅkā, roaming through every mansion (ValR 5:5ff.; RCM 5:5:3). In the ValR, he alternates between enthusiasm (5:10:12,17; 5:11:57), depression (5:4:24; 5:6:17; 5:10:2-3,23; 5:14:2), and hysterical states of agitation (5:5:1; 5:9:34; 5:10:2-9,24-25; 5:11:3-46), all of which easily lend themselves to the balladists' improvisations.[18] When he first lays eyes on sleeping Rāvaṇa, he is frightened (*paramodvigna*),[19] and at the sight of the Ten-headed's wife Mandodarī, he believes she is Sītā (5:8:49). For a moment, he rejoices in the manner of monkeys, kissing his tail, clapping his hands, climbing pillars, jumping on the floor (5:8:50); but he soon regains his poise (5:9:1), reasoning that without Rāma, Vaidehī would neither sleep, nor eat, nor wear ornaments, much less approach another male

(5:9:2-3). Therefore he concludes that this must be someone else (5:9:3). It suddenly occurs to Hanumān that he has transgressed the rules of *dharma* by looking at women and their features, and he feels repentant (5:9:34-36). However, when he considers the matter, he realizes there is no mistake on his part, for he had only been searching for Sītā, and where else could she logically be found except in the company of other females (5:9:40)? Thus, his intention was pure (*śuddha*),[20] and moreover, his mind, which is the prompter to good and evil, was unaffected (*na vaikṛtya)* by this sight (5:9:38-39). Though he decides that he has not in any way transgressed *dharma*, it may be inferred that he is feeling slightly guilty because his hitherto enthusiastic observations of the *rākṣasīs* suddenly become descriptions of deformities (5:10:4, 19).[21]

As he resumes the search, Hanumān soon becomes depressed and then fearfully agitated, completely loosing control of his *kapitva* (5:10:2-9). He worries about what may have happened to Sītā (5:10:2-4), he fears that Sugrīva will punish him (5:10:5), that his efforts have been in vain (5:10:6), that if he is too late, the monkeys will fast unto death (5:10:8), or that if they are still alive, the humiliation of his failure will be unbearable[22] (5:10:9). Realizing that the way to prosperity is not through despondency but through enthusiasm (5:10:10-11), he takes up the search again (5:10:12). In Rāvaṇa's inner apartments, he does not leave even a spot the width of four fingers unsearched (5:10:17). Nonetheless, his positive attitude gives way to depression (5:10:23) and eventually anxiety (5:10:24-25). He leaps over the wall of the famed aerial car (*Puṣpaka vimāna*)[23] and again begins to panic, but this time, more imaginatively than ever (5:11:3-46).

Even though Sampāti said that Sītā was in Rāvaṇa's palace, Hanumān has not found her (5:11:5). He assumes she must have died, and then enumerates all the possible causes of death: she may have fallen from Rāvaṇa's hands during the flight to Laṅkā (5:11:7), her heart may have stopped at the sight of the ocean (5:11:8), her abductor's speed may have been too great (5:11:9), Rāvaṇa may have suffocated Vaidehī as he was holding her (5:11:9), she may have fallen into the sea during a struggle with him (5:11:10), he may have eaten her (5:11:11), the *rākṣasīs* may have devoured her (5:11:12), she herself may have willingly died while meditating on Rāma (5:11:13) or calling on the Rāghavas and Ayodhyā (5:11:14). Having exhausted the above line of thought, Hanumān takes up another one. Whether Sītā is hidden, killed, or has died, he fears that he cannot tell Rāma due to the latter's love for her (5:11:17). Confused, Āñjaneya is unsure what to do (5:11:19). He wonders what is the use of going back to Kiṣkindhā without having found Vaidehī (5:11:21) and what Sugrīva and the Rāghavas will say (5:11:22). He worries that Rāma may die on hearing the news (5:11:23-24), as a result of which, Lakṣmaṇa will die (5:11:25), then Bharata and Śatrughna (5:11:26), the mothers (5:11:27), Sugrīva (5:11:28), Rumā (5:11:29), Tārā (5:11:30), Aṅgada (5:11:31), and the monkeys (5:11:32-36).

Hanumān concludes that his unsuccessful return would only cause a massive calamity for everyone (5:11:37), and therefore, he can under no circumstance go back (5:11:38). At least then the Rāghavas and the monkeys may live in expectation of his success (5:11:39), and he will not be the direct cause of their destruction (5:11:54). As for himself, he will either become an ascetic (5:11:40) or commit suicide (5:11:41-43). Having spewed the hysteria out of himself, he now employs his rational capacity in a more productive direction by considering the advantages of staying alive (5:11:47). For the sake of revenge, he could kill Rāvaṇa (5:11:49) or carry the latter to Rāma as an offering (5:11:50).

Though still full of grief (*dhyānaśokaparītātman*),[24] he decides to keep on searching until he can find Sītā (5:11:52), and begins with the Aśoka grove (5:11:55). Regaining enthusiasm, he vows to destroy all the *rākṣasas* and return Sītā to Rāma (5:11:57). With his grief washed away (5:11:58), he salutes Rāma, Lakṣmaṇa, Sītā, Rudra, Indra, Sugrīva, and others (5:11:59-60), and asks the *devas* for help (5:11:65-66). He then searches the Aśoka grove (5:12), finally seating himself in a tree (5:12:40), and looks for Vaidehī (5:13:1).

To summarize, Hanumān falls into four states of confusion: the first two may be taken as disappointments, the second one (5:6:17) more acute than the first (5:4:24); while the final two (preceded by his mistaking Mandodarī to be Sītā and his repentance for seeing women's features)[25] are full-blown states of mental hysteria, the last (5:11:3-46)[26] of which is a good deal worse than the one before it (5:10:2-9). The shorter state of depression (eight verses)[27] requires only three verses (5:10:10-12) to draw Hanumān back to enthusiasm, whereas the last one (forty-four verses)[28] requires no less than twenty verses (5:11:47-66) to recharge him. This frequent alternation between depression and enthusiasm, and particularly the last scene of mental agitation, demonstrates that Hanumān is, without the least scope for doubt, by nature, a monkey. However, though he seems completely to lose control, his train of thought still retains logical progression, and when he has almost reached the bottom of the pit, he still has the strength to turn around and start climbing up. His *kapitva* makes him particularly human, and yet his ability to pick himself up and start marching against the set current makes him superhuman, or at the very least a profoundly noble and strong human.

Irrespective of Āñjaneya's admirable courage in the midst of depression, Tulasī, as noted earlier, does not present his ideal devotee in this light, for the *bhakta* has neither cause to worry, nor the strength to draw himself out of the anxiety, since all is Rāma's. The author, therefore, takes a completely different line of development, presenting all-pervading Raghupati appearing behind every pillar and around every corner. As Māruti searches through Laṅkā, he comes upon a Hari temple (5:5:4), on the walls of which are painted the weapons[29] of Rāma (5:do.5). This is where he meets Vibhīṣaṇa, who is reciting *Rāmanāma* (5:6:1-2).[30] As on every other occasion when encountering beings other than monkeys, Hanumān assumes a human form.[31] As a *brahman* (*vipra*), he approaches Vibhīṣaṇa (5:6:3). The latter mistakes him for Raghupati (5:6:4), and when Māruti introduces himself, they develop close ties as fellow *Rāmabhaktas*.

Vibhīṣaṇa is initially concerned that Rāma may not be gracious to him because he is a *rākṣasa* (5:7:1-2), but he then realizes that proof of grace is already standing before him in the form of Hanumān (5:7:2-3). Māruti reassures him of Raghupati's love for all His servants (5:7:3) and gives his own example: though of most low birth (5:7:4), Āñjaneya has, in spite of that, received Rāma's grace (5:do.7).

Apart from being a fellow devotee, Vibhīṣaṇa, like Sampāti, is also an important source of information, for he tells Hanumān of Sītā's condition and exact whereabouts (5:8:2-3). *Bhaktas* can be found everywhere, and they are always helping one another.

The Recognition of Sītā

ValR 5:13
RCM 5:8:4—5:do.8

Upon arriving in the Aśoka grove, Tulasī's Hanumān, following the AdhyR (5:2:7-8), immediately recognizes Sītā (RCM 5:8:4). In the ValR, however, lengthy observation and deliberation are required to convince him of her identity (5:13). Seated in an Aśoka tree, he examines Vaidehī in three stages (5:13:18-25; 5:13:26-37; 5:13:38-49). In the first (5:13:18-25), he mostly notices her physical features, which are expressive of sorrow: her clothes are soiled (5:13:18, 20,25), she is weak and lean from fasting (5:13:18,22,25), she is sighing repeatedly (5:13:18), her eyes are full of tears (5:13:22), her hair is worn in a single braid (5:13:24),[32] and she has no ornaments (5:13:20). Again and again, Hanumān notes her profound sorrow (5:13:21,22,24) and also observes that she is surrounded by *rākṣasīs* (5:13:18,23). All this makes him suspect that she is Sītā, but he needs further evidence to be certain. So in the second stage of his examination (5:13:26-37), as in the first, he notices her physical features expressive of sorrow (the soiled clothes, the weakness, the sighing, the eyes full of tears, the lack of ornaments, and the fearful looks),[33] but this time, he marks more carefully the beauty he had merely noted before (5:13:19): her radiance (5:13:27,29), even though concealed (5:13:31,35), her face like the full moon (5:13:27), her lotus or fawn eyes (5:13:28,34), her eyebrows (5:13:27), her *bimba* red lips (5:13:28), her black hair (5:13:28), her breasts (5:13:27), and her slender waist (5:13:28). Hanumān also realizes that she has the same form as the woman abducted by Rāvaṇa (5:13:26), whom he and the four other monkeys[34] had seen from Mount Ṛśyamūka (4:6:9) as she was being carried away. Still, he is not satisfied that she is indeed Vaidehī (5:13:36-37) and enters upon the third and final stage of deliberation (5:13:38-49). Herein, his line of argument shifts from her sorrow and her beauty to logical reasoning confirmed by observation. It is to be noted here that contrary to previous statements (5:13:20,35), she is now said to have ornaments (5:13:39-42). It may be that as the reciters freely expanded the *Rāmakathā*, improvising at will, they added further reasons for the identification of this woman as Sītā, and in so doing, contradicted previous evidence.[35]

Hanumān notices those very ornaments which Rāma had mentioned to him as clues for recognizing Vaidehī (5:13:39-41). On the other hand, he notes that whatever adornments the woman being abducted threw down on Mount Ṛśyamūka, these same ones are not on this woman he is now examining (5:13:42). The rest, however, are still on her (5:13:42). Furthermore, the colour[36] and brilliance of the cloth she is now wearing is just like the upper garment that the monkeys saw falling down (4:6:9).[37] Lastly, he observes that her limbs are well-matched with Rāma's, as are Rāma's with hers (5:13:49). Only then is Hanumān certain that she must surely and without a doubt be Sītā (5:13:52), in search of whom he has leaped across the ocean and explored Laṅkā (5:14:12).

This scene highlights Āñjaneya's great caution and sense of responsibility. He neither wants to repeat his earlier misjudgement of someone else for Vaidehī (5:8:49), nor to spoil all his painful and anxious efforts by addressing the wrong person and then being discovered. The way in which he carries out his examination of Sītā demonstrates a clear, logical progression. Initially, he notes her internal condition of sorrow as reflected in her external appearance, then he deduces her previous external condition, and finally, logic confirms and brings together the two: she of concealed beauty who now grieves is the one whose radiance was previously apparent; that Sītā whom Rāma spoke of is this Sītā sitting under the tree.

Tulasī's Hanumān comes to the same conclusion, but in an instantaneous manner, for his heart is a direct pipeline to the Omniscient. Rather than first examining and then deciding, he knows and then observes, thereby confirming on the basis of knowledge. Furthermore, his observations of her physical features are very brief, extending only to her emaciated body and single braid (5:8:4). Clearly, it would be inappropriate for the eternal *brahmacārin* to dwell on a woman's appearance. The foremost *bhakta*, on the other hand, expands on her devotion to Rāma, in Whose lotus feet her mind is ever absorbed, and Whose qualities she ever repeats (5:8:4—5:do.8). While Vālmīki focuses on her sorrow, Tulasī concentrates on the cause thereof, her *bhakti*. In this way, Āñjaneya's attention turns from Sītā to Rāma.

REFERENCES

1. 5:2:33.
2. 5:2:37-38 is reduplicated in 5:28:37-38 when Hanumān is deliberating as to how he should approach Sītā. See p. 94.
3. RCM 5:do.3. The AdhyR (5:1:42) gives *sūkṣma*.
4. 5:2:46. Rāmānuja and Maheśvaratīrtha quote the *Amarakośa*: *otur viḍālo mārjāraḥ pṛṣadaṃśaka ākhubhuk ity amaraḥ*. Some MSS read *vṛṣadaṃśaka*, which commentaries, such as the *Tilaka*, define as "one who eats rats and mice", a cat: *vṛṣān mūṣakān daśatīti vṛṣadaṃśako mārjāras*. See crit. ed. footnotes. According to Winternitz 1904-20 (vol.1, p. 490, note 4), it could also be the size of a horse-fly.
5. Tessitori 1911, p. 286.
6. The AdhyR (5:1:53) specifies that this incident will mark the end of Rāvaṇa. This prediction is related to Nandin's curse of the king of the *rākṣasas* that he and his relatives will be destroyed by monkeys (ValR 7:16:13-15).
7. Cf. ValR 5:34:7.

8. Based on RCM lectures by Swami Tejomayananda.
9. Based on RCM lectures by Swami Tejomayananda.
10. Clearly, Hanumān's doubts about Rāma are receding further and further into the distance.
11. Wurm 1976, p. 107.
12. *Buddhist Mahāyāna Texts* 1894, part 1, pp. viii-ix.
13. Winternitz 1904-20, vol.1, p. 490, note 3.
14. *Buddhist Mahāyāna Texts* 1894, part 1, p.ix.
15. Three *chāṇḍas* as opposed to two- hundred and forty-six *ślokas* (ValR 5:4-9).
16. The crossing place for the ocean of *saṃsāra*. See Eck 1983, pp. 34-35.
17. *raghubīra sara tīratha sarīranhi tyāgi.*
18. Wurm 1976, p. 141.
19. 5:8:10. In 5:16:27, when Rāvaṇa enters the Aśoka grove, he is still afraid of him.
20. 5:9:42.
21. See Masson 1981, p. 358. Hanumān's perception of the women may well be connected to his lecherous, lewd character in Indonesia and Thailand, where he is said to marry Rāvaṇa's daughter, as also Lakṣmaṇa's, and to have affairs with Svayamprabhā, Vibhīṣaṇa's daughter, Mandodarī etc. (Bulcke 1959-60, p. 400).
22. Literally : "[With] the monkeys gathered around, what will elderly Jāmbavān say, and what will Aṅgada say?" (*kiṃ vā vakṣyati vṛddhaś ca jāmbavān aṅgadaś ca saḥ... vānarāś ca samāgatāḥ*).
23. ValR 5:11:1.
24. 5:11:51.
25. 5:8:49 and 5:9:34-41, respectively.
26. More precisely, it begins at 5:10:24.
27. 5:10:2-9.
28. 5:11:3-46.
29. Rather appropriate since *rākṣasas* are warriors.
30. In the ValR, Vibhīṣaṇa does not appear until Hanumān is being questioned by Rāvaṇa (5:50). Tulasī Dāsa gives him a rather high profile, for he has become a *Rāmabhakta*. After performing austerities (*tapas*) with his brothers Rāvaṇa and Kumbhakarṇa, in the ValR (7:10:27-28), followed by the AdhyR (7:2:18), he asks for the boon of *dharma*, whereas in the RCM (1:do.177), he requests for pure devotion to the Lord's lotus feet (*bhagavanta pada kamala amala anurāga*).
31. Two exceptions include the battle scenes and the meeting with Rāvaṇa. The obvious reason for Hanumān's transfigurations is that a human form is more impressive than that of a monkey. Therefore, in order to be taken seriously, he does not disclose his real identity until he has gained contact with the other parties, and he can then be

appreciated no matter what species he belongs to. His *vānara* form, however, does turn out to be an advantage in his mission in Laṅkā, for the *rākṣasas* do not pay too much attention to him precisely because he is a monkey, and as a result, his victory is easier. Also, leaping across the ocean is only possible for a *vānara*, and not for a human.

32. The single braid is indicative of a woman's separation from her husband (*Sri Ramacharitamanasa* 1949-51, note on 5:8:4).
33. 5:13:33-35.
34. The five are, according to 4:13:4, Sugrīva, Hanumān, Nala, Nīla, and Tārā (KKlf, vol. 2, note on 4:6:9).
35. In 5:15:30, she is again without ornaments.
36. Yellow, as noted by Hanumān in the first stage of his examination of Sītā (5:13:20).
37. 5:13:43,45.

12

THE INTERVIEW WITH SĪTĀ

ValR 5:14-38
RCM 5:9:1—5:17:3

Observation and Deliberation

ValR 5:14-28
RCM 5:9:1—5:so.12

In both texts, Hanumān is filled with pity at the sight of Sītā's plight (ValR 5:14:2,28; RCM 5:do.8). Vālmīki's Āñjaneya goes on to consider all that has been done, that is being done, and that will be done for her: because of Vaidehī, Vālin was destroyed (5:14:7), and the kingdom has gone to Sugrīva (5:14:11); for her sake, Hanumān leaped across the ocean and searched Laṅkā (5:14:12); and if on her account, Rāma should overwhelm the world, then that, according to Māruti, would be fitting (5:14:13). What amazing power has this poor creature whom he feels so sorry for! Wretched though her condition may be, the whole world appears to be revolving around her. Perhaps she is not so much a passive victim as a subtle provocative force compelling all beings to action. Were it not for her, there would be no *Rāmakathā*.[1] Thus, in her function as animator, it is not surprising that she appears more desirable than the three worlds (5:14:14). To add an ironic twist to this, in the AdhyR and the RCM, Vaidehī is not the real Sītā: prior to her abduction, the omniscient Rāma asked her to abide in fire until He, playing the part of a man (*naralīlā*),[2] had destroyed the *rākṣasas* (AdhyR 3:7:1-3; RCM 3:24:1). She therefore left behind only her reflection (*pratibimba*),[3] which now drives all creation to action. The Advaita Vedāntic overtones of the AdhyR, where Sītā as *māyā*[4] (Māyā Sītā)[5] can never be anymore than apparent, for she is neither real nor unreal,[6] are carried over in the *līlā* aspect into the RCM. With its dream-like dimensions, the external circumstances of Vālmīki's story have become the unfoldment of Raghupati's play, the hide-and-seek game of the RCM, in which Māruti enthusiastically and devotedly plays his part to perfection.

Though Hanumān is deeply distressed at the sight of her suffering, at the same time, he is delighted, to the point of shedding tears of joy, to have found her (ValR 5:15:30-32). Since this is a part of a later layer of the ValR, he mentally prostrates to Rāma and Lakṣmaṇa (5:15:31-32).

As Hanumān watches from the tree, Rāvaṇa, whom he still[7] fears (ValR 5:16:27), arrives (ValR 5:16:9; RCM 5:9:1). The latter presses Sītā (ValR 5:18; RCM 5:9:2-3), and she turns him down (ValR 5:19; RCM 5:9:3-5). In his anger, he wants to kill her (ValR 5:20:29; RCM 5:10:4), but is pacified by Mandodarī (ValR 5:20:37-38; RCM 5:10:4).[8] On his orders, the *rākṣasīs* torment Vaidehī (ValR 5:21-22; RCM 5:do.10) until one of them, Trijaṭā, recounts a prophetic dream she had, wherein Rāma defeated Rāvaṇa (ValR 5:25; RCM 5:11:1-4). Some MSS of the ValR[9] and Tulasī Dāsa (5:11:2) refer, in Trijaṭā's dream, to the burning of Laṅkā by Hanumān. Though this does not appear in the AdhyR account, a reference to Āñjaneya may be found in Rāvaṇa's dream of Rāma's monkey messenger watching from a tree (5:2:17).[10] It is to be kept in mind here that Āñjaneya sees and hears all that is taking place below him, and that he will therefore remember the prediction concerning him when his tail will be set on fire.[11]

At her wits' end, Sītā can only think of committing suicide (ValR 5:24,26; RCM 5:12:1-6). Hanumān realizes, since it would appear that he can read her mind, that it is high time he approach her before she follows through on her threat (ValR 5:28:12). In the ValR, this inevitably entails considerable deliberation (5:28:3-43), which, once again, expresses his monkey nature.

Hanumān begins by taking inventory of all he has thus far accomplished: he takes pride in having discovered her whom many thousands of monkeys searched for in all directions (5:28:3), for not having been detected as he moved through the city (5:28:4), for having ascertained the ability of the *rākṣasas* and the power of Rāvaṇa, and for having seen the city (5:28:5). Then, concerned as he is with right time, right place, and right action,[12] he first examines the last of these by considering the possible results of not consoling her. On the one hand, it would be a mistake for him to return immediately without comforting her (5:28:8) because she could kill herself (5:28:9,12,36), which would then render all previous efforts useless (5:28:15). On the other hand, if Rāma were to ask him for Sītā's message and Hanumān would have none, then the Rāghava would burn him up with his angry looks (5:28:13-14)—speculation which brings back to mind Āñjaneya's old fears and doubts concerning Rāma. Furthermore, there is yet another point which cannot possibly have escaped ethically-minded, duty-oriented Māruti: the Rāghava had not only asked him to find Vaidehī, but had also given him his own signet ring as a token of recognition (4:43:11). It is to be noted, however, that since the ring is a later interpolation,[13] this implication can only be inferred from the later layers of the *Rāmakathā*. In the early ValR, Hanumān logically deduces that even though he has not specifically been told to do so, he must speak to her, whereas in the more developed versions of the story, the ring becomes an explicit command (a "duty") for direct verbal communication. Having determined that he must address her, Āñjaneya also realizes that he must do so before the end of the night, giving as reason her inclination to commit suicide (5:28:12), but one might also add that he would be visible by daylight.

Now that he has decided on the right action and set the exact time, Hanumān ponders the conditions under which she should be addressed: they must be alone, without the *rākṣasīs* surrounding her (5:28:11). As for the form in which he should present himself, a miniature (*atitanu*) monkey might be appropriate (5:28:17). He must speak in the common language (*mānuṣī saṃskṛtā vāk*),[14] for if he uses chaste (*dvijāti*) Sanskrit, she will suspect him of being Rāvaṇa (5:28:18)[15] and cry out (5:28:21). At this point, Hanumān spins off into a frenzied flight of the imagination, conceiving of a disastrous sequence of events: hearing her scream out, the *rākṣasīs* will gather around her and Āñjaneya, and try to capture, if not kill him (5:28:22-23). Afraid of his leaping form (5:28:24) and the huge body which he will assume when threatened (5:28:25), they will call the guards (5:28:26). If Hanumān exhausts himself fighting with them, he may not have enough strength left to leap back across the ocean (5:28:28,34). Even worse, if they manage to catch him, they will tie him up, and Sītā will not benefit from his message (5:28:29). In fact, they may even kill her (5:28:30). If Āñjaneya is either captured or killed, there is no one capable, he believes, to achieve Rāma's objective (5:28:32). He therefore concludes that the uncertainty concerning the results of battle makes the potential conflicts undesirable (5:28:35).

Hanumān yet again[16] considers the necessary qualities of the doer; that is, keen awareness of right time and right place (5:28:37) and absence of conceit (5:28:38). Though he possesses both of these, there is still the question of right action (5:28:39). In the end, he decides to sing the praises of Rāma, which will not frighten Sītā (5:28:41), and on the contrary, will inspire her with confidence (5:28:43).

Tulasī Dāsa follows the AdhyR (5:3:3) in merely mentioning that Āñjaneya thought in his own heart (*hṛdayaṃ bicāra*).[17] He then immediately proceeds with the establishment of contact with Sītā and the subsequent *tête-à-tête*.

The Winning of Sītā's Confidence

ValR 5:29-34
RCM 5:so.12—5:do.13

Though the ValR and the RCM adopt the same basic methods to draw Vaidehī's attention and then her trust, the order in which the different means are employed varies. Vālmīki begins with the recitation of the *Rāmakathā* (5:29), then continues with Hanumān's presentation of exhaustive proof of his own identity (5:31-33), and concludes with the display of the ring (5:34). Tulasī Dāsa, on the other hand, initiates the process with the *mudrikā* (5:so.12), follows it up with an account of the Rāma story (5:13:3), and ends with Māruti's earnest self-identification (5:13:5).

Tulasī's Vaidehī, intent on committing suicide, has been praying to the Aśoka tree beneath which she sits to supply her with fire, for its young leaves bear the colour of flames (RCM 5:12:5-6). As if in response, Māruti now drops down Rāma's *mudrikā* (5:so.12). Initially she is thrilled (5:so.12), and then filled with sorrow, wondering how the invincible Rāghava could have been defeated, for the ring cannot possibly be a creation of *māyā*.[18] (She is certainly an authority on this last point because she herself is Māyā Sītā.)[19] In the G, which provides by far the clearest and most concrete illustration of the *mudrikā* 's instrumentality in its dual function as passport as well as contact between the Rāghava and Vaidehī,[20] Sītā directly addresses the ring, and it, in turn, replies that Rāma is well, thereupon pointing out Hanumān's presence in the tree (5:4).[21] To relieve her confusion, Āñjaneya begins to recount Rāma's praises and the *Rāmakathā* (RCM 5:13:3; G 5:4). Vālmīki (5:29:2-9) and the AdhyR (5:3:4-15) quote the full account from a description of Daśaratha to Hanumān's own discovery of Vaidehī. The praise of the Rāghava, as it appears in Vālmīki's version, may be understood in two ways: if it is taken as part of the early text, then Āñjaneya, who is riddled with doubts about Rāma, is simply trying to gain Sītā's confidence so as to accomplish his mission; if, however, it is taken as part of the later text, then Hanumān, who no longer harbours any ill feelings towards the divine Rāghava, is merely expressing his own devotion to the Latter. In other words, it is a case of diplomacy versus devotion, the ideal *dūta* versus the ideal *bhakta*.

Whereas Vālmīki's Sītā now looks up and sees Hanumān in the Aśoka tree (5:29:12), Tulasī's Vaidehī does not try to spot him, but rather asks that he show himself (5:13:4). He, in turn, approaches her from the back, for she is seated with her back to him (5:13:4), and solemnly swears by Rāma (*satya sapatha karunānidhāna kī*) that he is the Latter's messenger, addressing her as "mother Jānakī" and explaining that he has been entrusted with Raghupati's *mudrikā* (5:13:5). Tulasī's description of Hanumān's approach of Sītā displays a gradual progression: first in the tree, then through the intermediary of Rāma's ring, after which from behind, and finally from the front.[22] These stages serve to emphasize not only Hanumān's *brahmacarya*, but also Sītā's spotless purity and devotion to Rāma, for she never takes her eyes from her own feet and her mind from Rāma's feet (5:do.8).

So while in the RCM it takes very little to convince her of Hanumān's sincerity, for swearing by Rāma carries far more weight here than in the ValR, in the latter text, the situation is more complex. In order to facilitate the examination of the persuasion of Vaidehī by Vālmīki's Hanumān, it may be helpful first to summarize the process: after hearing the *Rāmakathā* and seeing the monkey in the tree, Sītā doubts her own perception (5:30,32); Āñjaneya reassures her with guess questions,[23] then introduces himself, gives his message, and comforts her (5:31-32); when she questions him, Māruti answers in great detail (5:33), and finally produces the ring (5:34).

Initially, Sītā believes she is dreaming (5:30:2), but realizes that cannot be the case because she is not and has not been sleeping (5:30:5). Furthermore, the sight of a monkey in dream is inauspicious (5:30:4; 5:32:21), yet she is receiving happy news (5:32:21). Then she thinks she is hallucinating (5:30:6; 5:32:19) because she has been concentrating on Rāma and consequently sees what is in accord with her mental preoccupation[24] (wishful thinking[25]). She soon realizes, however, that she is neither mad nor imagining things because an illusion has no form (5:30:7). Moreover, as proof of her sanity, she clearly sees who she is and who the monkey is (5:32:23). Well, if she is neither dreaming nor hallucinating, the monkey may be Rāvaṇa in disguise (5:32:9,24).

Seeing her predicament, Hanumān tries to handle the situation as delicately and tactfully as possible so as not to destroy everything when he has come this far. He salutes her with joined palms (5:31:1)[26] and asks who she is (5:31:2,8), stating that he perceives her to have the marks of a queen

(5:31:9) and that he therefore concludes that she must be Sītā, which conclusion he requests that she confirm (5:31:10). As expected, she does (5:31:12), and this provides Āñjaneya with final and definite corroboration of his own deductions (5:13:52). Also, by conveying his awareness of her suffering (5:31:3), he gains her confidence.[27]

Hanumān then introduces himself as Rāma's messenger and gives, in brief, Rāma's message: his welfare, his concern for her welfare, and Lakṣmaṇa's greetings (5:32:2-4). As Āñjaneya comes closer and closer to her, again she becomes suspicious and frightened (5:32:9-24), and he soon realizes that he has not yet convinced her of his identity (5:32:26). He tries to comfort Sītā by telling her that Rāma is always thinking of her (5:32:35) and that she will soon see him (5:32:36). There seems very little else that Hanumān can do, but fortunately she takes the initiative to question him on where he met Rāma, how he knows Lakṣmaṇa, and how an alliance was concluded between a man and monkeys (5:33:2). She also asks him to describe the distinguishing marks of the two Rāghavas (5:33:3-4).

Āñjaneya immediately jumps at this opportunity, exhaustively answering her questions in no less than seventy verses (5:33:6-75). He begins with the last one because it is dearest to Vaidehī's heart. If this passage is taken as an early layer of the ValR, then this is shrewd manipulation made possible by his psychological insight. Just as he had previously appealed to Sugrīva's emotions (4:28:22),[28] he now uses the same tactic on Sītā. If, however, this is understood as a later layer of the ValR, then he is expressing his own *Rāmabhakti*.

Although he was asked to describe both of the Rāghavas' features, Lakṣmaṇa is alloted one verse (5:33:21), while Rāma receives thirteen verses (5:33:8-20). Whether it is a case of shrewdness or devotion, Hanumān knows Vaidehī's heart. He depicts Rāma's spotless character (5:33:8-12,20), his glory (5:33:9), his profound knowledge of statecraft, archery, the *Vedas* and the *Vedāṅgas* (5:33:13-14), the right time and place (5:33:20),[29] as well as his physical features (5:33:15-19).

Āñjaneya then goes on to describe where he met Rāma and Lakṣmaṇa and how that, in turn, led to the alliance between a man and monkeys (5:33:22-47), thereby answering her other questions (5:33:2). He further recounts Rāma's fulfilment of his end of the agreement (5:33:48) and identifies himself as the *dūta* of both Rāma and Sugrīva (5:33:49). Afterwards, he narrates the latter's efforts to uphold his side of the alliance up to Hanumān's own discovery of Sītā (5:33:50-64). He loyally omits the monkey king's lapse in duty,[30] thereby presenting him in a more favourable light. Again he identifies himself and his task (5:33:66) in the hope that this time she will believe him. He assures her that Rāma will soon kill Rāvaṇa (5:33:72), and to give her more confidence, recounts his own parentage (5:33:73-75) and his desire for her trust (*viśvāsārtha*),[31] which she finally gives him (5:33:76-78). Hanumān then pulls out his final trump, the ring (5:34:2), seeing which, there cannot remain even the slightest speck of doubt in her mind.

The question may be raised as to why Vālmīki's Māruti did not present the ring first, as in the RCM, instead of taking the trouble of verbally convincing her. As discussed earlier,[32] the ring is a later interpolation, and therefore the above reference to it has conveniently been appended to the end of Āñjaneya's arguments and descriptions. Furthermore, it is meant merely as a confirmation and final proof of Hanumān's sincerity and identity,[33] for even in the more developed layers of the ValR it has not yet gained the symbolic status which it holds in the RCM, where it embodies *Rāmakāja* (*Rāmakārya*) as *rāmeṇa kārya*[34] and thus must come first.

In the ValR, Sītā recognizes Hanumān as the heroic (*vikrānta*), resourceful (*samartha*), and wise (*prājña*) envoy of Rāma, who leaped across the ocean as if it were the mark of a cow's hoof, and whom she considers as no ordinary (*prākṛta*) monkey due to his fearlessness of Rāvaṇa and lack of mental confusion (5:34:6-8).[35] In the AdhyR (5:3:38) she sees him as intelligent (*buddhimat*) and as a *Rāmabhakta*, the latter of which becomes *the* quality in the RCM (5:do.13; 5:14:1; 5:17:1), where, based upon it, Vaidehī develops a relationship of affection to him.[36] Precisely because it is through Tulasī's Māruti that Rāma speaks to her, Āñjaneya has become the bark for her who was drowning in the ocean of separation (*viraha*) from the Lord (5:14:1).

While in the ValR (5:34:9) and the AdhyR (5:3:38-39), Sītā decides that Hanumān must be a fit person for her to speak to since he is sent by Rāma, the question of fit or unfit does not arise in the RCM, for *bhakti* overrides *dharma*. Furthermore, Vālmīki's Vaidehī estimates him to be, generally speaking, a fit messenger (5:34:10), which point is not only obvious to Tulasī Dāsa, but the consideration thereof would be symptomatic of a lack of faith in Rāma, extended to uncertainty concerning His devotees.

The Comforting of Sītā

ValR 5:34-38
RCM 5:14:1—5:17:3

While Vālmīki's Sītā wonders whether or not Rāma still loves her and will rescue her (5:34:19), Tulasī's Vaidehī assumes that He has indeed forgotten her (5:14:4), and though all-merciful (*komalacita kṛpāla*), He has, in her perception, become merciless (*niṭhurāī*).[37] Whereas Vālmīki strives to keep the situation at the level of right conduct (*dharma*), Tulasī breaks all barriers of social correctness, transcending them through *bhakti*: Sītā sheds tears (5:14:4), despairs (5:14:2-4), and even makes accusations of indifference against her spouse (5:14:2). This should not, however, be construed as Vaidehī's lack of faith in Raghupati, but rather as Tulasī's way of showing her great love for Him (*viraha bhaktī*).

As the two Sītās show different symptoms and express different priorities (*dharma* versus *viraha bhaktī*), Hanumān must apply two different remedies in accordance with the given situations. While in the RCM he must comfort Vaidehī primarily at the emotional level and only secondarily at the logical level, in the ValR, the latter comes to the forefront.

Tulasī's Hanumān assures Sītā that both brothers are well (5:14:5), except that Rāma, Whom he refers to as "the abode of great mercy" (*sukṛpā niketā*) in order to counter her accusation that the compassionate One has become careless (5:14:2), is sorrowful due to her sorrow because He loves her twice as much as she loves Him (5:14:5). Māruti then urges her to compose herself and listen to Rāma's message (5:do.15), which, actually, Āñjaneya has just given her in a nutshell form so as to calm her down in one stroke.

Vālmīki's Hanumān, on the other hand, simply assures Sītā that if Rāma had known her whereabouts, he would already have destroyed the *rākṣasas* and rescued her (5:34:32-33; 5:35:20). This argument is also used in the RCM (5:16:1), but only after the delivery of Raghupati's message. The reason for Tulasī's delay is the obvious absurdity of the Omniscient's ignorance of her location. The fact that the RCM mentions the argument at all may be explained in at least three ways: Tulasī may be acting in deference to Vālmīki; the statement is accurate at the level of Rāma's play (*līlā*); it is a last resort to calm down the *māyā*-bound Sītā (Māyā Sītā).[38]

Filled with devotion (5:do.14), Tulasī's Hanumān quotes Rāma's message (5:15:1-4). Though this is not taken word-for-word from a previous scene, and the ideal *bhakta* would under no circumstance take liberties with the speech of the Lord, one possible explanation is that Raghupati is directly speaking to Sītā through His perfect instrument. In his total humility, Āñjaneya disappears, thereby providing the opportunity for a private and highly intimate conversation where no third party intrudes.[39] In this manner, Tulasī asssures the faithfulness of the message which is genuinely Rāma's rather than Hanumān's version thereof.

Vālmīki's Māruti does not directly quote the Rāghava, for a quote was never given which could now be quoted. Therefore, Hanumān is not so much giving Rāma's message as a description of the latter's love for Sītā. He assures her of the Rāghava's imminent arrival in Laṅkā and of the certain defeat of the *rākṣasas* (5:34:32-34), swearing that she will indeed see Rāma (5:34:36-37). Characteristic of a monkey, he swears by the mountains, fruits, and roots, as he had sworn by Rāma Himself in the RCM (5:13:5), where his *kapitva* has turned into *bhaktatva.* Vālmīki's Hanumān goes on to express Rāma's sorrow and its different manifestations (5:34:35,39-44), and assures her that the Rāghava is thinking of ways to rescue her (5:34:44).

In the RCM, Rāma expresses, through Hanumān, how all that He had hitherto (until His separation from Sītā) found pleasing has become its opposite (5:15:1-2). He then elaborates on the subject of their mutual love (5:15:3-4), which Māruti had touched on earlier (5:14:5).

In the ValR, while Sītā is relieved of her sorrow, she is also distressed at hearing of Rāma's anguish (5:34:45). In the RCM, however, the question of grief does not arise, for she is so overcome with love that she loses consciousness of her body (5:15:4). It would seem that Hanumān has performed his self-effacing duty almost too well, for he is now obliged to tell her to compose herself and to find the strength to do so by remembering Rāma (5:15:5). He then assures her of Raghupati's certain victory over the *rākṣasas* (5:do.15—5:16:1).

At this juncture, the ValR (5:35:21-68), followed by the AdhyR (5:5:6-8),[40] presents an incident symptomatic of Hanumān's *kapitva* (ValR 5:35:31). Eager to do as much as possible to relieve both Sītā's and Rāma's sorrow, Āñjaneya offers to take Vaidehī back to the Rāghava (ValR 5:35:21-22; AdhyR 5:5:6). She refuses, giving a series of excuses: she argues that Hanumān is too small (*alpaśarīra*) to carry her across the ocean (ValR 5:35:32), that she is afraid of the speed and height of the flight (ValR 5:35:45-46), that she is worried about the possible failure of the attempted escape (ValR 5:35:48-56,58), and that she fears for Rāma's consequent reputation (ValR 5:35:57; AdhyR 5:5:7-8) and for her own purity (ValR 5:35:62). Blinded by his excessive zeal, Āñjaneya becomes uncharacteristically slow-witted, not realizing that Vaidehī's first three reasons are only pretexts for her unwillingness to allow herself to be touched by anyone but the Rāghava, whose honour (*yaśas*) is her primary concern. Hanumān does not grasp this until she spells it out for him.[41]

Āñjaneya counteracts her first argument by manifesting his colossal form (ValR 5:35:37), and somewhat offended, boasting of his capacity to carry the whole of Laṅkā together with Rāvaṇa across the ocean (ValR 5:35:39).[42] This is matched in the AdhyR and the RCM by a scene wherein Sītā's doubts concerning the ability of small monkeys to defeat mighty *rākṣasas* (AdhyR 5:3:63-64; RCM 5:16:3-4) are resolved when Hanumān reveals his frightening, powerful, and heroic mountain-like form (AdhyR 5:3:65; RCM 5:16:4). Tulasī also takes this opportunity to point out that the size of the monkeys is irrelevant, for with the Lord's power, even a very small snake is capable of eating Garuḍa (5:do.16). The *kapis* themselves have no *bala* or *buddhi* of their own; everything comes from Rāma. In other words, Sītā has asked the wrong question, but for Tulasī's purposes, it is the right question.

When slow-witted Hanumān finally comes to perceive the problem with his proposal, he has a certain amount of explaining to do. He is not, however, in any way ashamed of himself, but rather delighted at Sītā's words (ValR 5:36:1). Though he may have been a little too eager and impetuous, his motives were pure, as they were based on his affection (*sneha*) for Rāma (ValR 5:36:7) and his desire to reunite Sītā with the latter (ValR 5:36:9). He insists that there was no other reason (ValR 5:36:9). Vaidehī cannot possibly be angry with Hanumān because of his innocent and kind heart. His reaction here is clearly a part of a later layer of the ValR, as he refers to Rāma as *guru* and to his relationship to him as one of *sneha* and *bhakti* (5:36:9).

The RCM does not show Hanumān in a "monkey-ish" light, and therefore, for the most part, omits his improper suggestion. What the text does contain is a simple explanation as to why the action cannot be carried out, and thus why it cannot even be proposed: Rāma has not ordered Māruti to bring Sītā back (RCM 5:16:2). In this way, Tulasī avoids any impropriety or impurity. Also, since Hanumān knows Rāma's purpose, in the service of which he has incarnated as monkey, if he were to suggest doing everything himself, that would imply the futility of the Lord's birth. In *Rāmakāja* (*Rāmakārya*) as *rāmeṇa kārya,* Raghupati does carry out some of His work directly (without Hanumān's instrumentality).

While the RCM (5:27:1) saves Māruti's request for a token of recognition from Sītā until after the burning of Laṅkā, Vālmīki (5:36:10) places it prior to his encounters with the *rākṣasas* and his adventures in the city. Tulasī's Vaidehī, following the ValR, offers her crest-jewel (ValR 5:36:52; RCM 5:27:1) and the account of the crow incident (ValR 5:36:12-32; RCM 5:27:3),[43] whereas Vālmīki's Sītā also includes the story of the arsenic forehead mark (5:38:5).[44]

Vālmīki's Hanumān gives Sītā more words of reassurance and encouragement (5:37:13-16,32-45; 5:38:13-16), and as he is about to leap back across the ocean, he suddenly feels that there is more (*alpaśeṣa*) for him to accomplish (5:38:24). This is clearly a later layer of the ValR, for a doubting Āñjaneya would not willingly go out of his way to do more than is required of him. Tulasī's Hanumān, however, takes a slightly different route because he already knows, or better yet, spontaneously acts out (Rāma acts out through him) the next step. After Sītā has blessed him (5:17:1-2), recognizing him as a beloved of Rāma (*rāmapriya*),[45] he repeatedly prostrates to her (5:17:3), and following the AdhyR (5:3:67), asks her permission to eat the fruits of the Aśoka grove (5:17:4). Seeing his *buddhi* and *bala,*[46] which implies her knowledge not only of his true intent, but also of his possession of the necessary qualities for success therein, she permits it (5:do.17).

REFERENCES

1. See Dimmitt 1982.
2. RCM 3:24:1.
3. RCM 3:24:2. The AdhyR (3:7:2) uses the word *chāyā,* meaning "shadow" or "reflection".
4. 1:4:18.
5. 3:7:4.
6. See Śaṅkarācārya's commentary on *Brahma Sūtra* 1:4:3 (referred to in *The Brahma Sūtra* 1960).
7. See ValR 5:8:10.

8. In the ValR, Rāvaṇa is pacified by a *rākṣasī* called Dhānyamālinī, which may be another name for Mandodarī. Some MSS of the ValR specifically use the name Mandodarī (see crit. ed.).
9. Crit. ed., passage 615 inserted following 5:25:23. This is clearly a later reference because the burning of Laṅkā is considered to be an interpolation (Jacobi 1893, pp. 31-37).
10. In the AdhyR (5:2:15-20), Rāvaṇa desires to hasten his own death at Rāma's hands, and therefore, based on his dream, he hurries to the Aśoka grove, where he wounds Sītā with his harsh words because he believes the monkey will then inform Raghupati (Who will consequently come sooner). Rāvaṇa's only motivation for abducting Vaidehī is his devotion to the Lord (7:3:29-59;7:4:9-11).
11. This, of course, applies only to the later layers of the ValR and to the RCM. See p. 119.
12. E.g. 4:28:14-15.
13. See p. 49.
14. 5:28:17.
15. Rāvaṇa appeared to her as a *brahman* and therefore spoke to her in chaste Sanskrit when he came to abduct her (3:44).
16. See 5:2:37-38 referred to on pp. 79-80.
17. RCM 5:do.12.
18. 5:13:1-2.
19. See RCM 3:24:1-2.
20. See pp. 49-50.
21. In the Bahadur translation (*Complete Works of Goswami Tulsidas* 1978-80, vol. 3), see G 5:222.
22. Tulasī Dāsa does not make a special note of this last stage, but it has clearly taken place by the time Sītā asks Hanumān how monkeys such as him, evidently referring to his small size, could fight mighty *rākṣasas* (5:16:3).
23. Hanumān used this technique in his first encounter with the Rāghavas. See pp. 26-27.
24. 5:30:6.
25. 5:32:22.
26. According to an inserted verse (crit. ed., passage 660 inserted before 5:31:1), he has now descended from the tree.
27. Wurm 1976, pp. 124-25.
28. See p. 39.
29. This is quite a compliment when it comes from one so deeply concerned with *kāla* and *deśa* (e.g. ValR 5:2:37-38).
30. See p. 37.
31. 5:3:75.
32. See p. 49.
33. The AdhyR follows the ValR sequence.
34. See pp. 48-49.

35. Actually, Hanumān has thus far been afraid of Rāvaṇa (5:8:10; 5:16:27), though, as will be seen, this is only a temporary condition. As for states of confusion, he has experienced quite a number of them already (e.g. 5:11).
36. Refer to *Bṛhadāraṇyaka Upaniṣad* 2:4:5 quoted on p. 38.
37. 5:14:2.
38. From a symbolic point of view, Sītā is *māyā* (see p. 91) and therefore not subject to it, but when she is personified in an embodied form, her form itself being an expression of *māyā*, she becomes *māyā*-bound.
39. See p. 50.
40. In the AdhyR, the passage occurs following the burning of Laṅkā.
41. If Sītā is understood to be the animator, the *śakti* of Rāma, then her excuses are intended to prevent Hanumān from taking her back so as to force the Rāghava to acts of heroism. See Dimmitt 1982, p. 220.
42. Cf. ValR 5:35:22.
43. Once when Rāma and Sītā were living on Mount Citrakūṭa, a crow (Indra's son Jayanta) pecked Vaidehī. Angered, the Rāghava invoked the Brahmā missile from a blade of grass and sent it after the culprit. The crow flew through the three worlds in search of refuge, but finding none, took shelter at Rāma's feet. The missile, however, could not go in vain (*mogham*), and therefore, at the crow's suggestion, it destroyed the latter's right eye. (This episode appears only in the northern recension of the ValR [*The Rāmāyaṇa of Vālmīki: Bālakāṇḍa* 1984, p. 38].)
44. Once when Sītā's *tilaka* disappeared, Rāma replaced it with an arsenic (*manaḥśilā*) mark.
45. 5:17:1.
46. See also RCM 4:30:2; 5:2:1,6;5:do.2. In this case (5:do.17), though his *bala* will enable him to defeat many of the *rākṣasas*, it is his *buddhi* which will ultimately procure him an interview with Rāvaṇa (see pp. 113ff.). Therefore, *buddhi* precedes *bala*.

13

THE DESTRUCTION OF THE AŚOKA GROVE

ValR 5:39-46
RCM 5:17:4—5:20:2

Whereas Vālmīki (5:39:1-12) presents a lengthy description (twelve verses) of Hanumān's deliberation concerning his next move, the AdhyR prefixes any such thought (two verses)[1] with hunger and the appeasement thereof (5:3:67-68), and the RCM then omits all speculation, maintaining only the hunger (5:17:4). Thus, the originally well planned destruction of the Aśoka grove gradually changes into an instinctive Rāma-inspired act. Though the intention, the obtaining of information and the conveying of a message, is the same, the stratagem initially arises from the level of the mind of an ideal *saciva-dūta*, and later, from the level of the heart of an ideal *bhakta*.

Though he has fulfilled what the Rāghava and Sugrīva ordered, Vālmīki's Āñjaneya feels there is still something more for him to do (5:38:24; 5:39:2). After all, a skillful emissary is one who, apart from accomplishing the entrusted assignment, also achieves much more, so long as it is not opposed to his main task (5:39:5). One option is to attempt to win Rāvaṇa over through the only means which would impress him; that is, force (5:39:2-4). If the king of the *rākṣasas* sees many of his powerful kinsmen killed, he will likely give in (5:39:4). If that fails, Hanumān will at least have determined the strength and the strategies of the enemy (5:39:7), besides having eliminated some of the bravest warriors[2] and instilled fear in the demons. Āñjaneya thereby makes extensive preparations for Rāma's ultimate attack.[3]

The means to confrontation, he reasons, is by destroying the grove (5:39:9-11). For that purpose, he becomes fierce like the wind and expresses his terrible prowess (*bhīmavikrama*) by striking down the trees with his thighs (5:39:13). In the RCM, however, true to his original request from Sītā (5:17:4), Māruti engages in eating fruits while uprooting trees (5:18:1). Whereas Vālmīki's account describes a premeditated violent act, Tulasī's is of the nature of *līlā* (*Rāmalīlā*). Just as Hanumān had playfully leaped to the top of Mount Mahendra (RCM 5:1:3), he now revels in joy, filled with that same natural and unassuming ease. Battles with *rākṣasas* begin, not because he intentionally attacks them, but because they stand in the way of his enjoyment of the fruits of the garden. Furthermore, the encounters take the form of effortless pushing away rather than blood-thirsty confrontation.

As Vālmīki is interested in developing Hanumān's powerful warrior aspect, he elaborates on the *rākṣasa*-encounters a good deal more (5:40-46) than Tulasī (5:18:2—5:20:1) does. He repeatedly refers to Āñjaneya's pugnacity (e.g. 5:39:17; 5:40:34), his roaring in eagerness (e.g. 5:40:28; 5:41:10) while awaiting his prey (5:41:10; 5:42:5; 5:43:16; 5:44:39; 5:45:19, 39). His huge body (5:40:4; 5:41:4) moving through the sky (5:40:29; 5:41:15; 5:43:9-10; 5:44:21), the sound of his tail striking the ground (5:40:28), his threats and boasts, such as his ability to outdo even one thousand Rāvaṇas (5:41:8),[4] frighten the inhabitants of Laṅkā (5:40:1). The *rākṣasīs*, knowing that Sītā has spoken to him (ValR 5:40:6; AdhyR 5:3:76),[5] and seeing that in his rampant destruction he has not even touched the place where she sits (ValR 5:40:17; AdhyR 5:3:72), question her (ValR 5:40:6-7; AdhyR 5:3:73), but without avail (ValR 5:40:8-10; AdhyR 5:3:74). They run to inform Rāvaṇa (ValR 5:40:11; AdhyR 5:3:75), suggesting that the monkey may be a messenger of Indra, Kubera, or Rāma (ValR 5:40:15), and urge him to punish Hanumān (ValR 5:40:20). At this stage, the king of the *rākṣasas* begins to send various parties to fight Āñjaneya.

Māruti operates from the gate-tower of Laṅkā (ValR 5:39:17), repeatedly returning to his post every time he defeats some of the demons, and in challenge awaits, like Time (Kāla), the arrival of others (ValR 5:40:34; 5:43:16;

5:44:39; 5:45:39). In total, he has seven encounters: eighty thousand *kiṅkaras* (ValR 5:40:23-32);[6] one hundred guards (ValR 5:41:11-15); Prahasta's son Jambumālin (ValR 5:42:1-17);[7] seven sons of ministers (ValR 5:42:19—5:43:14); five generals (ValR 5:44:2-38); and Rāvaṇa's sons Akṣa (ValR 5:45:1-36) and Indrajit (ValR 5:46:1-36). While the AdhyR (5:3:78-98) omits the guards and Jambumālin, the RCM reduces the list to four conflicts; that is, the watchmen (5:18:2), the *rākṣasa* warriors (5:18:3), Akṣa (5:18:4), and Indrajit (5:19:1—5:20:1).

The reaction of Vālmīki's Rāvaṇa to Hanumān is, at first, anger, which grows every time he has to send out another party, for he is thoroughly irritated that a mere monkey is effortlessly killing mighty demons. His hurt pride, however, prevents him from realizing how very powerful an opponent he stands against. Following the defeat of his ministers' sons, he finally begins to sense trouble, though he is careful enough to conceal his feelings (*saṃvṛtākāra*).[8] Therefore, when he dispatches the next group (the generals), he advises them to be most cautious, for he no longer considers Hanumān to be a mere monkey, but perhaps a creation of Indra through his *tapas* (5:44:6), or an emissary of the *nāgas, yakṣas, gandharvas, devas,* and *ṛṣis* (5:44:7-8). He urges the generals not to underestimate Āñjaneya (5:44:9), as he himself has done, for he has seen powerful monkeys, such as Vālin, Sugrīva, and Jāmbavān (5:44:9-10).[9] Moreover, the abilities of those monkeys are no match for Hanumān's speed, splendour, prowess, intelligence, strength, enthusiasm, and capacity to take any form at will (5:44:11). He concludes that Āñjaneya must be a great creature (*mahatsattva*) in monkey form (5:44:12). Clearly, fear has begun to penetrate Rāvaṇa's heart. When prince Akṣa is killed, his father is filled with great fear (*mahadbhaya*),[10] which leads him to warn powerful Indrajit of the opponent's intelligence, great strength, and courage (5:46:9). Some MSS insert two verses[11] wherein Rāvaṇa explains the impossibility of overcoming Hanumān by any and every means: even an army is futile, for Āñjaneya has the ability to destroy large numbers at a time. Thus, as Māruti's powers are gradually magnified by the balladists, so are Rāvaṇa's esteem and fear of him. The climax is reached in Tulasī's *Kavitāvalī*[12] (5:9), wherein the king of the *rākṣasas* is overcome with despondency as he watches Āñjaneya burn down Laṅkā. Rāvaṇa compares his brilliance (*pratāpa*) to that of one hundred million suns,[13] describes his frightfulness (*karālatā*) as surpassing that of Death himself, and depicts his great stature (*baṛāī*) as exceeding the Dwarf's. "If his messenger is of this kind, then what need the Master come?"[14]

As for Hanumān's battle opponents, their attitudes towards him vary according to their own greatness: the first five of Vālmīki's parties are either instantly killed, or they flee from him in fear; Akṣa is amazed (*vismita*) and filled with respect (*bahumāna*);[15] while Indrajit grasps that Āñjaneya cannot be killed (*avadhya*).[16]

As for Hanumān's reactions to his opponents, the one to Akṣa is particularly noteworthy. He is delighted at the latter's prowess and even has respect for him (5:45:24). He praises Akṣa's courage and self-control (5:45:27-28), and considering him an accomplished warrior, Āñjaneya is reluctant to kill him immediately (5:45:26). He slays him only due to necessity, in order to accomplish his own purpose, for Hanumān realizes that the war lust which is allowed to grow is like fire which spreads if neglected (5:45:29). He thereby admits Akṣa's capacity to defeat him unless quick measures are now taken.

After fighting with Hanumān for some time and realizing that the latter cannot be killed (ValR 5:46:33), Indrajit considers how to bind him (ValR 5:46:33).[17] When force and *māyā* have failed (RCM 5:19:4-5), as a last resort he directs Brahmā's missile (*Brahmāstra*) at Hanumān (ValR 5:46:34; RCM 5:do. 19). While Vālmīki's Āñjaneya cannot be killed by such a fearsome weapon (5:46:35), Tulasī's Māruti cannot even be bound by it (5:20:2). His invulnerability is based on a boon from Brahmā, according to which none of the Creator's weapons have the power to harm him (ValR 4:65:25; 7:36:19). Consequently, in the ValR and the AdhyR, though he is bound (ValR 5:46:36; AdhyR 5:3:98), he has the capacity to release himself (*vimokṣaśakti*),[18] and even if he chooses not to do so, the effect of the bondage is nullified in the presence of other binding (ValR 5:46:46). Hanumān considers this bondage as a blessing from Brahmā himself (ValR 5:46:37), for it will allow him to meet Rāvaṇa (ValR 5:46:42,45; AdhyR 5:4:2). Therefore, he determines that he must submit to it (ValR 5:46:39-40), or appear to be bound (ValR 5:46:49), even when he is released as a result of further binding by the *rākṣasas* (ValR 5:46:44-46). Through his *buddhi,* he outwits the enemy. Indrajit alone is aware of his release and the great threat he represents to all the *rākṣasas* (5:46:47-48,51).

In the RCM, Māruti surrenders to the weapon for the same reason, the service of Rāma (5:20:2), but also for the sake of maintaining the *Brahmāstra's* reputation of boundless greatness (5:do.19). The changes which Tulasī has made in this scene highlight Hanumān's enhanced power, invincibility, and at the same time, profound humility.

REFERENCES

1. 5:3:69-70.
2. According to the AdhyR (6:1:24), Hanumān kills one quarter of the *rākṣasas.*
3. Wurm 1976, p. 131.
4. Cf. AdhyR 5:4:30.
5. Actually, this is something they were not supposed to know, for their awareness of Hanumān's presence could have placed the entire enterprise at risk (ValR 5:28:22-32). He himself had made every effort to avoid being seen by them (5:28:11).
6. As indicated in ValR 5:40:23, the *kiṅkaras* are a class of *rākṣasas.*
7. Jambumālin in 5:42:1,6,12,17; but Jambumāli in 5:42:15,18.
8. 5:44:1.
9. Though Jāmbavān has come to be considered a bear, the ValR, as noticed in this passage, does not draw a decisive line between *vānaras* (*haris*) and *ṛkṣas.* See Goldman 1989.
10. 5:45:37.
11. Crit. ed., passage 1011 inserted following 5:46:10.
12. Henceforth abbreviated to K.
13. Cf. *Bhagavad Gītā* 11:12.
14. *jāko aiso dūta so sāhaba abai āvano* (K 5:9). Translation by F.R. Allchin in *Kavitāvalī* 1964.
15. 5:45:8.

16. 5:46:33.
17. In the RCM (5:19:1), Rāvaṇa had ordered his son to do exactly that, specifying, contrary to the ValR (5:46:12), that Hanumān should not be killed so that his identity and origin may be established.
18. ValR 5:46:40. In the AdhyR (5:4:2), his bondage lasts only for a little while (*kṣaṇamātrasaṅgama*).

14

THE INTERVIEW WITH RĀVAṆA

ValR 5:47-50
RCM 5:20:3—5:25:2

As Hanumān is beaten and dragged before Rāvaṇa (ValR 5:46:50,55), the *rākṣasas* gather around (RCM 5:20:3), wondering who he is (ValR 5:46:53) and asking that he be killed (ValR 5:46:54). While in the ValR he admires and praises Rāvaṇa's prowess and splendour (5:47:16-18), in the RCM he merely notes it without being in the least affected by it (5:20:3-4). Vālmīki's Hanumān recognizes the enemy's power as so great that if it had not been channelled into *adharma*, it could have been sufficient to protect even the realm of the gods (ValR 5:47:18; 5:57:3).

The fear which the ValR's Āñjaneya had earlier experienced at the sight of Rāvaṇa (5:8:10; 5:16:27) is transmuted into anger (5:47:1), which is then diplomatically controlled (e.g. 5:49:2). In Tulasī's case, there never was any question of fright because total surrender to the Lord includes the surrender of all feelings of anxiety. When Raghupati Himself does His own work, what need Hanumān fear? Therefore, when all beings, including the *devas* and the protectors of the directions, tremble before Rāvaṇa, Māruti is completely unaffected, just as Garuḍa amidst serpents (5:20:4).

As for Rāvaṇa's reaction to Hanumān, in the ValR it is cautious, and in two inserted verses thereof,[1] fearful, for he wonders whether it is not Śiva himself, by whom he had been cursed when he shook Mount Kailāsa, or Bāṇa.[2] In the RCM, Rāvaṇa is more foolish, laughing at and humiliating Māruti and then falling into dejection upon remembering his own son's death (5:do.20).

Vālmīki's Rāvaṇa, as is befitting for a king, has his ministers interrogate Hanumān,[3] while in the RCM he himself directly addresses the "captive" (5:21:1). The line of questioning is much the same with the occasional variation: the purpose of his presence in Laṅkā (ValR 5:46:58), his identity (ValR 5:48:5-7; RCM 5:21:1), the place where he has come from, his reason for destroying the Aśoka grove and threatening the *rākṣasīs* (ValR 5:48:3). Instead of this last query, Tulasī, following the AdhyR (5:4:5), has Rāvaṇa asking about the offence for which Hanumān killed the *rākṣasas* (RCM 5:21:2). Though on the surface the RCM interrogation appears to take Āñjaneya more seriously, the ministers of the ValR may simply not wish to expose their concern regarding the latter's destructive achievements, and therefore, they reduce them to the ravaging of a garden and the frightening of demonesses.

Furthermore, the RCM paves the way for the glorification of Rāma by questioning the identity of the one by whose *bala* Māruti destroyed the grove (5:21:1). This is somewhat parallel to the ValR (5:48:7), where Prahasta doubts Hanumān is a monkey, for his power is not a monkey's power. Also, in order to underline Āñjaneya's fearlessness, Tulasī makes Rāvaṇa refer to it and explain it by Hanumān's lack of acquaintance with the king of the *rākṣasas* (5:21:1-2). Not only is this suggestion extremely unlikely, for the Ten-headed has terrorized the world enough (RCM 1:181:2—1:do.182b), but it is also profoundly insulting, for even the *devas* tremble before him (RCM 5:20:4). Āñjaneya's obvious boldness shocks the demon, who now threatens him with death (RCM 5:21:2) so as to inspire fear into him. Clearly, Hanumān's behaviour is in direct contrast to that of almost anyone else whom the Ten-headed has ever encountered.[4]

In the ValR, Hanumān tells the ministers he is the *dūta* of the king of the monkeys (5:46:59), and he begins his reply to Prahasta by denying all of the latter's inaccurate guesses concerning his own identity: he is sent neither by Indra, nor by Yama, Varuṇa, or even Viṣṇu (5:48:10-11).[5] Furthermore, he is indeed a *vānara* (5:48:11). In the RCM (5:21:2—5:do.21), following the AdhyR (5:4:8), Māruti defines himself in terms of his relationship to Rāma, and in the form of a discourse, describes the Latter's different aspects and functions:

Hanumān is the envoy of Him Who is *Brahman, Īśvara,* and *Rāmāvatāra*; by Whose *bala, māyā* brings forth numberless universes, Viṣṇu creates, Śiva destroys, and Śeṣa upholds the cosmos (5:21:2-3); Who incarnates in various forms (5:21:4); and Who is Rāma (5:21:4-5). In this explanation, Māruti also relates Rāvaṇa's might to the Lord's *bala*, by an iota of which, the king of the *rākṣasas* was able to conquer the entire world (5:do.21). Thus, Hanumān inflicts a blow on Rāvaṇa's pride, apart from instructing the latter and replying to his questions.

Since the demon is hard-hearted, Tulasī's Āñjaneya keeps chipping at the latter's ego, reminding him of his bitter defeats at the hands of Sahasrabāhu and Vālin (5:22:1).[6] Though the pungent tone and the ironic remarks are meant to pierce through Rāvaṇa's vanity, the coating is so thick that they do not quite demolish his arrogance, for he is still able to laugh (5:22:1). In spite of being humiliated in front of all his subjects and suffering the death of a son, he cannot bring himself to take a monkey seriously.

In the AdhyR (5:4:12) and the RCM (5:22:2), Hanumān tells Rāvaṇa that he ate because he was hungry, and in so doing, according to his monkey nature, broke off branches and trees. When the *rākṣasas* attacked him, he fought back only for his own protection (ValR 5:48:13; AdhyR 5:4:13; RCM 5:22:3). In the ValR (5:48:14) he goes on to explain that thanks to a boon from Brahmā, gods and demons cannot bind him with any weapon.[7] In order to meet the king of the *rākṣasas,* he has willingly submitted to the *Brahmāstra* (ValR 5:48:15; AdhyR 5:4:14), though he was no longer bound upon being tied with ropes (ValR 5:48:15). Tulasī's Hanumān, however, does not boast of his boon, of his own power, or of his intelligence, whereby he has devised and then carried out his plan to meet Rāvaṇa. On the contrary, in deference to the Lord, he is not ashamed of being bound (where there is no ego, there can be no humiliation), for he only desires to carry out *Rāmakāja* (5:22:3). Having merged his individuality in the Lord, if his own personal "defeat" is a means to accomplish Raghupati's work, then that is glory rather than shame. This, of course, brings to mind the subject of Hanumān's low birth, which is actually so elevated because it is exactly the form needed to carry out Rāma's work.[8] It is due to Āñjaneya that all monkeys are worshipped in India today.

While in the ValR (5:48:16) and the AdhyR (5:4:14), Hanumān asks Rāvaṇa to hear what he has to say, for it is conducive to the Ten-headed's welfare, in the RCM (5:22:4) he not only begs Rāvaṇa with joined palms to listen to his advice, but also gives a further instruction for the auditing process; that is, the giving up of pride (*māna taji*). As the devotee of the Lord of all beings, Māruti is concerned for all beings, even for the worst of them, such as Rāvaṇa. That is why he pleads with the latter to give heed while there is still time and opportunity. Being wise, he is also a teacher (AdhyR 5:4:15-26) capable of spotting the root of the problem; that is, pride. If ego is given up, Rāvaṇa can be persuaded to worship Rāma. If, however, this crucial instruction is disregarded, there is no hope for peaceful reconciliation and forgiveness.

In the ValR, instead of simply accusing Rāvaṇa of abducting Sītā, as Tulasī's Āñjaneya does (5:do.21), or even directly linking the act to him, Hanumān merely mentions Vaidehī's disappearance (5:49:7) in his account of the entire *Rāmakathā* up to his own search in Laṅkā (5:49:4-14). He is very respectful and cautious in regard to the king of the *rākṣasas*, and even goes so far as to claim that Sugrīva is concerned about Rāvaṇa's welfare (5:49:2). This may be explained by Vālmīki's emphasis on right conduct, by Hanumān's skill as a diplomat, and by the latter's limited respect for and admiration of Rāvaṇa's power and wealth. In Tulasī's version, however, *bhakti* overrides *dharma*, and Māruti is completely unaffected by the demon's aura or possessions.

While Vālmīki's Hanumān is trying to convince the Ten-headed to return Sītā (5:49:19), Tulasī's primary concern is to make Rāvaṇa worship Rāma (5:22:4; 5:23:1; 5:do.23), and only then to return His spouse (5:22:5). The arguments used by Āñjaneya to achieve his desired ends are different precisely because his respective objectives differ somewhat. While *dharma* is one of two major arguments in the ValR, the RCM mentions it only peripherally, and even there, in the devotional context of reverence to sages. Whereas Tulasī refers to the high family honour which sage Pulastya's grandson is in the process of disgracing (5:22:4; 5:23:1), Vālmīki refers to the Ten-headed's knowledge of *dharma* (5:49:15), both of which are intended to shame him into right conduct befitting his lineage and his person, respectively.

When the reference to personal *dharma* fails, Vālmīki's Hanumān describes the effect of actions which are opposed to *dharma*; that is, complete destruction (*mūlaghāti*).[9] He also explains the impossibility of overcoming the fruits of *adharma* through the previous results of *dharma*, which, incidentally, in Rāvaṇa's case, have already been used up (5:49:27-28). Since Āñjaneya knows and perhaps even sees from Rāvaṇa's reaction that the threat of death and destruction is most effective in reaching him, he pursues this argument from different directions. By pointing out that both Lakṣmaṇa (5:49:17) and Rāma (5:49:18,32,35) are invincible, he reminds the *rākṣasa* of the elder Rāghava's slaying of Vālin. This last incident should frighten the Ten-headed, for Vālin had once humiliated him (7:34).[10] Rāma has even taken a vow to destroy Sītā's abductor (5:49:31). Hanumān also indicates that Rāvaṇa's boon of invincibility at the hands of all beings excludes men and monkeys (5:49:25-26).[11] Āñjaneya claims that he himself is capable of single-handedly destroying Laṅkā (5:49:30). He also elaborates on the theme of Sītā as death itself: she is like a five-hooded serpent (5:49:21), the embodiment of the destructive force which will devastate the whole of Laṅkā (5:49:33), and even now, the city is afire with her effulgence[12] (as will be materialized in the burning of Laṅkā[13]). Together, these arguments are forceful enough to make Rāvaṇa react.

In the RCM, Hanumān takes a completely different line of argumentation, focusing above all on the greatness and invincibility of Rāma (5:22:5; 5:23:4), which are balanced by His compassion (5:do.22). Just as in the AdhyR (5:4:22-24), he therefore urges Rāvaṇa to worship the Lord (5:22:4; 5:do.23), if not selflessly, then either for the benefits thereof (uninterrupted rule of Laṅkā)[14] or from fear of the consequences of not doing so (the short-lived wealth and lordship of one who is opposed to Rāma).[15]

Hanumān's counselling takes different forms because of Rāma's gradually unfolding figure. The more developed his image, the more emphasized is his divinity. Therefore, greater and greater respect is due to him until it is no longer good enough merely to return Sītā, or even to apologize, for He is now to be worshipped whole-heartedly.

Parallel to the divergent nature of Āñjaneya's advice are Rāvaṇa's two somewhat diverse reactions. Since Tulasī's Hanumān has offered him a sermon, he laughs at the thought of a monkey playing the part of a *guru* (5:24:1). When Āñjaneya offends him again (5:24:2), he is, just as in the ValR (5:49:36; 5:50:1) and the AdhyR (5:4:27), overcome with rage (5:24:3) and orders that the monkey be executed (5:24:3). The AdhyR (5:4:30) adds another interruption by Hanumān, wherein the latter claims that even crores (*koṭis*) of Rāvaṇas cannot equal him, for, as Rāma's *dūta*, his power is boundless (*apāravikrama*) and by implication unobstructable. Furious, the king of the *rākṣasas* is about to kill Āñjaneya himself when he is stopped by his brother Vibhīṣaṇa (AdhyR 5:4:32). The latter, who in the ValR (5:50:3) is said to be well acquainted with and established in right conduct, and in the RCM (5:6:2ff.), a devotee of Rāma,[16] protests that to kill a messenger is opposed to statecraft (ValR 5:50:6; AdhyR 5:4:32; RCM 5:24:4).[17] Furthermore, Vālmīki's Vibhīṣaṇa explains that there can be no gain in killing Hanumān, for the latter is only following orders, and therefore, the one who sent him should be killed (5:50:10). Another disadvantage in doing away with Āñjaneya is that he will not be able to inform his master of Rāvaṇa's whereabouts, and then the demon will lose his opportunity to punish Rāma (AdhyR 5:4:33). What other messenger could possibly reach Laṅkā (ValR 5:50:12)? The same arguments are put in the mouth of Tulasī's Rāvaṇa, who is eager to witness Raghupati's power (*prabhutāī*).[18] In this manner, the RCM avoids putting any blemish on the *bhakta* Vibhīṣaṇa, who would never dream of suggesting to his brother to kill Rāma. At best, Vibhīṣaṇa can only recommend, as he has done in the other texts (ValR 5:50:6-7; AdhyR 5:4:34), another punishment for Hanumān (RCM 5:24:4).

Some MSS of the ValR have a few more verses wherein Rāvaṇa reflects that Āñjaneya may be Viṣṇu's *tejas* in the form of a monkey, or even the Supreme *Brahman*, and he is filled with anger at the thought.[19] In the RCM (5:24:5) he regains his calm and laughs, considering how silly it is for so mighty a *rākṣasa* to get angry over an insignificant monkey. Rāvaṇa then instructs that Hanumān's tail be set on fire (ValR 5:51:3; RCM 5:do.24), for since the tail is most precious to monkeys, the experience should be rather humiliating (ValR 5:51:4; AdhyR 5:4:37).

While Vālmīki does not present any reaction on Hanumān's part to the order, Tulasī (5:25:2) displays the latter's delight, for Māruti considers that Śāradā (Sarasvatī) has proved helpful to him. This discrepancy may be explained by referring back to the mention of the burning of Laṅkā in Trijaṭā's account of her dream, which Hanumān heard as he was sitting in the Aśoka tree (5:11:2).[20] At the time, he could not have known how he would be able to burn down the city, but now, as his tail is about to be set on fire, he understands. Furthermore, as Śāradā is the goddess of learning, he attributes his understanding to her.

REFERENCES

1. Crit. ed., passage 1031 inserted following 5:48:1.
2. Bāṇa is the eldest son of Bali and a favourite of Śiva. In the *Kamba Rāmāyaṇa* (5:13:70), Rāvaṇa extends the list to include Nārāyaṇa, Brahmā, and Śeṣa, insisting that Hanumān must be one of them in disguise (Aiyar 1951, p. 183).
3. In the first instance (5:46:58), a number of unnamed ministers, and in the second (5:48:2-3), only Prahasta. The AdhyR (5:4:5-6) has Prahasta alone.
4. Three exceptions may be cited: Sahasrabāhu (RCM 6:24:8; *Shri Ramacharitamanasa* 1989, p. 891), who was the king of Kārtavīrya, once captured Rāvaṇa and brought him home for his own amusement until sage Pulastya (Rāvaṇa's grandfather) rescued the captive; when Vālin (RCM 6:do.24; note on 5:22:1 in *Sri Ramacharitamanasa* 1949-51) was performing his twilight (*sandhyā*) ritual, the Ten-headed

tried to capture him from behind, but the powerful monkey caught him and held him under his armpit for six months until Brahmā came to the demon's rescue; Rāvaṇa once descended to the nether world in order to conquer Bali (RCM 6:24:7), but children tied him to the stables, played with him, and beat him until Bali took pity on him and let him go. Furthermore, the ValR (7:32-33) recounts how the king of the *rākṣasas* was captured by Arjuna and released at Pulastya's request.

5. Obviously an earlier passage since Rāma was not yet identified with Viṣṇu.
6. See note 4 above.
7. Cf. AdhyR 5:4:14.
8. Similarly, Kākabhuṣuṇḍi chooses ever to remain in the low form of a crow, for in it he obtained *Rāmabhakti* (RCM 7:95:4).
9. 5:49:16.
10. For the story of Vālin's humiliation of Rāvaṇa, see note 4 above.
11. See also ValR 1:14:13-14; 7:10:17-18.
12. 5:49:35. This illustration brings back to mind Sītā's everything but passive position. See p. 91.
13. 5:52.
14. 5:23:1.
15. 5:23:3.
16. See p. 89, note 30.
17. *Arthaśāstra* 1:16 (Kane 1946, p. 128). P.V. Kane (pp. 127-31) also notes a *dūta's* two-fold duty as a messenger and a spy. H.D. Sankalia (1982, pp. 90-91) explains that since Hanumān is now acting as a spy in Laṅkā, Rāvaṇa's treatment of him and Vibhīṣaṇa's attitude are most considerate.
18. 5:25:1.
19. Crit. ed., passage 1059, lines 3,7-8 inserted following 5:50:17. See variant reading for line 3.
20. As noted earlier, certain MSS of the ValR also refer to the burning of Laṅkā. See p. 92.

15

THE BURNING OF LAṄKĀ[1]

ValR 5:51-53
RCM 5:25:2—5:do.26

As the *rākṣasas* are winding cloth around Hanumān's tail (ValR 5:51:6; RCM 5:25:2), he swells (ValR 5:51:7; RCM 5:25:3) to such an extent that in Tulasī's account, all the cloth, ghee, and oil in the whole of Laṅkā are used up. Whereas in the ValR he is propelled by anger (5:51:9), in the RCM it is all play (*khelā*).[2]

When his tail is set on fire (ValR 5:51:8), Vālmīki's Hanumān angrily strikes the *rākṣasas* with his burning tail (5:51:9). At first, he wants to break the ropes that bind him and fight the demons (5:51:11-12), but for Rāma's sake (*rāmasya prītyartham*), he decides to endure the humiliation (5:51:12), for as he is being dragged through the city, he will have the opportunity to examine the details of its fortifications by daylight (whatever he had noted earlier[3] was during the night).[4] In the RCM, however, where the parade through Laṅkā precedes the ignition of the tail (5:25:4),[5] there is no mention of spying out the fortress' defensive-offensive possibilities, for Hanumān is playful (5:25:3) rather than strictly militarily shrewd, and if he does notice something, then it is part of his play as a spontaneous and joyful expression of Rāma's will, manifesting the unfoldment of the divine plan in preparation for the ultimate battle.

In the ValR, when the *rākṣasīs* inform Sītā of Hanumān's lot (5:51:20-21), she implores Agni to act on him as a cooling agent (5:51:22-27). As soon as her prayer is answered (5:51:28), Āñjaneya notices that the fire is not burning him (5:51:29) and attributes this to Rāma's power, Sītā's benevolence, and Vāyu's friendship with Agni (5:51:31,33). Just as the Ocean and Mount Maināka are interested in Rāma's affairs (5:1:75-

118),[6] so is the Fire (5:51:32). In the RCM, Śiva explains to Pārvatī that Hanumān was not burned because he is the messenger of Him Who created fire itself (5:26:4).

While Vālmīki's Hanumān leaps onto the city gate and diminishes his form in order to get out of his bonds (5:51:34-36), in the AdhyR (5:4:41-42) and the RCM (5:25:4-5), he first takes a minute form, and as soon as he is freed, leaps to Laṅkā's attics.[7] Whereas in the ValR (5:52:2) he must consider his next step, in the AdhyR (5:4:41), while he is being dragged through the streets, he already has a stratagem in mind. Resuming his mountain-like (ValR 5:51:37; AdhyR 5:4:42), sky-reaching appearance (RCM 5:do.25), which is now, according to Tulasī's K, more horrific than ever (K 5:4-5,8-9), he jumps from mansion to mansion, setting the entire city, apart from Vibhīṣaṇa's house (AdhyR 5:4:46; RCM 5:26:3) and of course Sītā's spot, aflame with his tail (ValR 5:52:6; AdhyR 5:4:43-44; RCM 5:26:1). The K describes the fire he sets as inextinguishable even by the clouds of deluge, which when invoked by Rāvaṇa, only serve to increase it and finally turn and flee (5:19).

> Terrifying that mighty tail, like some net of flames it was, as though Death himself had stretched out his tongue, all Laṅkā to envelop... On the lanes, and in the markets, on the roof-terraces and the housetops, by every door and wall was the monkey to be seen. Above ..., below...,—the monkey! This way... that way...,—the monkey! It was as if the monkey were filling the three worlds. Closed they eyes, then there before them, in the mind's eye opened standing![8]

With Laṅkā as the altar, his tail as the ladle, the *rākṣasas* as oblations, and his mighty roars as "svāhā", Hanumān performed the sacrifice (K 5:7), and "the ten directions were wreathed with the matted garlands of the flames."[9]

With the work completed, Āñjaneya now jumps into the ocean in order to extinguish his tail (ValR 5:52:17; RCM 5:26:4), and suddenly, Vālmīki's Hanumān is filled with doubts (5:53:2-26). Since the amount of deliberation preceeding the burning of Laṅkā was minimal (5:52:2-5), it is now compensated for by twenty-five verses of highly nervous speculation. It dawns upon him that he should have considered the possible consequences of his actions. Overcome as he was with anger, he may have defeated the very purpose of his mission (5:53:6), for when Laṅkā was burnt, Sītā also must have been burnt (5:53:4,7). In despair, he thinks of committing suicide (5:53:9), fearful of facing Sugrīva and the Rāghavas (5:53:10).[10] Ashamed and depressed at having manifested his *kapitva* (5:53:11) and terrified of the potential results, he enters upon an uncontrolled flight of mental gymnastics, which, though briefer, is almost identical to an earlier one wherein he was discouraged at not having found Sītā (5:11:23-37).[11] If she is dead, the Rāghavas, Sugrīva and his relatives, Bharata and Śatrughna will die, all the subjects will be overcome with sorrow (5:53:13-15), and he himself will be the destroyer of the world, all because his anger has gotten the better of him (*roṣadoṣaparītātman*).[12] But as usual, all is not lost, for he continues to reflect, and just as he thought himself into the problem, he now thinks himself out of it. He considers that Sītā is protected by her *tejas*, in which case she cannot be burnt by fire, for fire cannot burn fire (5:53:18). In fact, Agni cannot even as much as touch her (5:53:19). Then he remembers that he himself, through Rāma's power and Vaidehī's benevolence (5:51:31,33), was unscathed by the fire, and so how could Sītā possibly be harmed (5:53:20-22)? Becoming more and more encouraged, Hanumān goes so far as to claim that she is capable of burning fire itself (5:53:23). His deductions are confirmed by the celestial bards (*cāraṇas*),[13] but he decides to see her again in order to eliminate any further traces of doubt in his own mind (5:53:28).

Sītā praises Āñjaneya (ValR 5:54:3), he bids her farewell (ValR 5:54:8), and sets off across the ocean (ValR 5:54:18). In the RCM, this is the stage at which she gives him tokens of recognition for Rāma (5:27:1,3). She then despairs at Hanumān's departure (5:27:4), and he, having comforted her, starts off (5:do.27).

REFERENCES

1. According to Jacobi (1893, pp. 31-37), this scene is a later interpolation, a comic relief.
2. 5:25:3.
3. 5:4-9.
4. 5:51:13.
5. The AdhyR follows the order of events of the ValR.
6. See pp. 71-72.
7. In the AdhyR (5:4:42), following the ValR (5:51:35), he leaps up to the city gate.
8. *bāladhī bisāla bikarāla jvālajāla mānauṃ laṅka līlibe ko kāla rasanā pasārī hai / ... bīthikā bajāra prati aṭani agāra prati paṃvari pagāra prati bānara bilokiye / adha ūrdha bānara bidisi disi bānara haiṃ mānahu rahyo hai bhari bānara tilokiye // mūnde āṅkhi hīya meṃ ughāre āṅkhi āge ṭhāṛho...* (K 5:5,17).
   Translation by F.R. Allchin in *Kavitāvalī* 1964.
9. *lapaṭa karāla jvālalajālamāla dahūṃ disi* (K 5:16).
   Translation by F.R. Allchin in *Kavitāvalī* 1964.
10. Cf. 5:11:22.
11. See p. 84.
12. 5:53:16.
13. 5:53:26.

16

HANUMĀN'S REPORT TO RĀMA

ValR 5:62-66
RCM 5:29:1—5:34:3

Hanumān flies across the ocean, like an arrow released from the bow (*jyāmukta iva*).[1] As he catches a glimpse of Mount Mahendra in the distance, he roars so loudly that the monkeys on the seashore hear him and rejoice (ValR 5:55:10-11,14).[2] When he arrives, Vālmīki's Āñjaneya immediately confirms their presumptions of his success by declaring that he has seen Sītā: *dṛṣṭā devī* (5:55:24). In the RCM, on the other hand, they need only look at his contented face and effulgent body (5:28:2). Tulasī Dāsa, following the AdhyR, communicates much greater urgency in reaching Rāma with the news by omitting Vālmīki's lengthy exchange (5:55-57) between Hanumān and the members of the southern expedition, wherein Māruti reports on his mission. On their way to Mount Prasravaṇa, the monkeys stop in Madhuvana, Sugrīva's garden, and while indulging in its fruits and honey, they destroy it and beat the guards (ValR 5:59-60; RCM 5:28:4). When news of the monkeys' activities reaches Sugrīva, he realizes they have accomplished their task, for otherwise they would not dare to make such havoc (ValR 5:61:23; RCM 5:29:1). In the ValR, the king of the monkeys automatically assumes Hanumān has seen Sītā, for in his inordinate affection for and admiration of his *saciva*,[3] he assumes that Āñjaneya alone could accomplish the work (5:61:16).

Upon arriving in the presence of Rāma, Vālmīki's Hanumān immediately assures him of Sītā's chastity and well-being (5:62:38). By having the *dūta* speak first, the author underlines Āñjaneya's threefold position as leader of the expedition, accomplisher of all that is to be accomplished, and conscientious messenger, who wishes immediately to put the

Rāghava's concerns to rest. Tulasī Dāsa, however, is intent on emphasizing Māruti's humility on the one hand, and Raghupati's omniscience on the other, and therefore does not allow the devotee to speak until the latter is called upon to do so (RCM 5:30:4). The RCM thus shifts the focus from the messenger to the One Who sent him.

Following this statement by Vālmīki's Hanumān, the exchange between Āñjaneya and Rāma follows the same basic framework in both texts: the monkeys speak; Hanumān is asked to speak; Hanumān speaks. The brief account of Sītā's condition by the ValR's monkeys (5:63:3-4) finds its correspondence in two passages of the RCM, wherein the *kapis* inform Sugrīva of Hanumān's doings (5:29:3), and then Jāmbavān notifies Rāma of the same (5:30:3), thus underlining Āñjaneya's greatness, whose achievements "one thousand tongues cannot describe".[4] Just as Tulasī had presented a steady progression in Māruti's approach of Sītā,[5] he now uses the same technique, advancing from Sugrīva, through the monkeys, to Rāma, through the army's elder wise man figure.

While in the RCM (5:30:4), Raghupati asks Hanumān about Vaidehī, in the ValR (5:63:6), the monkeys, upon themselves being asked by Rāma, request Hanumān to explain. Tulasī displays a much closer relationship between Āñjaneya and Rāma than Vālmīki ever does, for he is functioning at the level of *bhakta* and *Bhagavān*, wherein the *bhakta* shares in and expresses *Bhagavān's* nature and being.[6] While Vālmīki's Rāma, delighted at the news of Sītā, looks at Māruti with great respect (*mahābahumāna*),[7] Tulasī's Raghupati gazes at him with eyes full of tears (*locana nīra*) and body bristling (*pulaka ati gātā*)[8] and strokes his head (5:33:1). Whereas in the ValR (6:1:12) he later embraces Hanumān, in the RCM (5:30:4; 5:33:2), the embrace is immediate— even before Āñjaneya has spoken a single word—and repeated.

In Tulasī's version, Māruti's account of Vaidehī's condition fails to mention how she is being persecuted by Rāvaṇa and the *rākṣasīs*, concentrating rather on her devotion to Rāma, for that is the main point, and in fact, the only point. The ValR and the AdhyR give a report of her sad plight in Rāvaṇa's city at the hands of the *rākṣasīs* (ValR 5:63:9-14; AdhyR 5:5:37-38). Vālmīki also provides a much fuller description of the tokens of recognition (ValR 5:63:18-21; 5:65:2-17,30) than appears in the RCM, which refers only to the crest-jewel (5:31:1).[9] Both texts speak of Sītā's loyalty to Rāma (ValR 5:63:14, 17,24; RCM 5:do.30—5:do.31) and her concerns that he has failed to rescue her due to some fault of hers (ValR 5:65:18-23; RCM 5:31:2-4). In fact, in the RCM, she points out that her only fault is her survival in spite of her separation from Rāma (5:31:3), but this she attributes to her eyes, which seek only to see Him (5:31:4).[10]

Prompted by his own obvious distress over Sītā's suffering, Hanumān now urges Rāma to act quickly (ValR 5:63:25; RCM 5:do.31). Based on Vaidehī's wish to preserve the Rāghava's glory (*yaśas*),[11] Vālmīki's Āñjaneya incites him to accomplish the task which will bring him that glory (5:66:11).

Rāma is delighted at Hanumān's report, and in the ValR, followed by the AdhyR (5:5:60; 6:1:2-6), cannot praise him enough: no one, even in thought—apart from Āñjaneya, that is—could possibly succeed in such a great and arduous mission, for while only Garuḍa and Vāyu have the ability to cross the ocean, no being from any class whatsoever is capable of both entering and exiting Laṅkā (ValR 6:1:2-5). Rāma therefore concludes that none is equal to Hanumān in prowess and strength (ValR 6:1:5). He highlights the latter's accomplishment by contrasting the highest type of individual (*puruṣottama*), who succeeds at a difficult task (ValR 6:1:7), carrying out both the expressed and unexpressed purposes of the master[12]— Āñjaneya's case—with the lowest person (*puruṣādhama*), who, though competent, does not do what is asked of him (ValR 6:1:8).[13] This passage is briefly paralleled in the RCM (5:33:3) by Rāma's question to Hanumān as to how he was able to burn Laṅkā. This inquiry expresses wonder at Māruti's achievements, thus underlining the greatness of the *bhakta*, while the latter's response (5:33:4-5) re-emphasizes Raghupati's predominance, for in giving all credit to Rāma (5:33:5), it identifies the devotee's greatness as the Lord's greatness. Āñjaneya thus prays for unceasing devotion (*anapāyanī bhagati*) to Him (5:34:1) Whose favour and power enable even cotton to burn a submarine fire (5:do.33).

Rāma is unable to repay Hanumān for such a great service (ValR 6:1:11; AdhyR 5:5:60; RCM 5:32:3-4), for, as a later verse of the ValR points out,[14] in order to be in a position to do so, Āñjaneya would have to be assailed by misfortune so as to be rescued from it. Since Rāma would certainly not wish him harm, it is more desirable that the Rāghava should remain incapable of paying him back for this favour. He now embraces Hanumān (ValR 6:1:12, AdhyR 5:5:61; RCM 5:33:2), and in some MSS of the ValR as well as in the AdhyR (5:5:61), gives Māruti his all (*sarvasva*).[15] Tulasī's Āñjaneya is overcome with devotion and falls at the feet of the Lord (5:do.32), Who with difficulty succeeds in lifting him up (5:33:1-2). Raghupati, in the words of the K (6:55; 7:19), has enslaved Himself (*hātha bikāne*) in His devotee's love. It may also be added that He has "further" enslaved Himself, for His human incarnation itself presupposes this condition, since *bhakti*, as Tulasī explains (RCM 1:116:1), is the force which moves the unqualified (*nirguṇa*) *Brahman* to become qualified (*saguṇa*).

Having received Hanumān's report, the Rāghavas and the monkeys set out to Laṅkā, where the battle begins. Fighting valiantly, they all distinguish themselves.

REFERENCES

1. ValR 5:55:9. Cf. 5:1:36; 5:12:4. See also AdhyR 5:1:3 and RCM 5:1:4, referred to on p 71.
2. In the AdhyR (5:5:11-12), the monkeys hear him roar all the way from Laṅkā.
3. See p. 47.
4. *sahasahuṃ mukha na jāi so baranī* // (5:30:3).
5. See pp. 95-96.
6. *Bhakta* and *Bhagavān* are from the Sanskrit root *bhaj*, meaning "to share" or "to partake of".
7. 5:62:40.
8. 5:32:4.
9. The AdhyR (5:5:53) mentions both the crest-jewel and the crow incident.

10. Literally, "for their own benefit" (*nija hita lāgī*), which both the Geeta Press translators and R.C. Prasad (*Shri Ramacharitamanasa* 1989) interpret as the desire of the eyes to behold Rāma.
11. ValR 5:35:57.
12. S.V.S. Sastri 1949, p. 290.
13. Some MSS add a middle category for the ordinary person (*madhyama nara*), who, though capable, does nothing more than what he is told (see crit. ed.).
14. Crit. ed., passage 776 inserted following 7:39:18.
15. Crit. ed., passage 775 inserted following 7:39:18. In the ValR verse, the word used is *prāṇas.*

17

THE BRINGING OF THE MEDICINAL HERBS[1]

ValR 6:61,89
RCM 6:54:4—6:62:2

Hanumān's most well-known exploit during the battle in Laṅkā is the bringing of the medicinal herbs from the Himalayas. In the ValR (6:61, 89) and the AdhyR (6:5:71-74; 6:6:32—6:7:39), the scene is repeated twice, while in the RCM (6:54:4—6:62:2), the two accounts are amalgamated into one and modified according to Tulasī's purposes.

In Vālmīki's first passage (6:61), almost the entire army, including both Rāghavas, is lying unconscious.[2] The second passage (6:89) records only Lakṣmaṇa's swooning, for it may reflect a later stage of the ValR, wherein Rāma, as Viṣṇu's *avatāra*, is undefeatable. Therefore, Tulasī follows, for the most part, the latter account.

Further evidence for the antecedence of the first scene can be found in the passage itself. After Indrajit has crushed the entire army (ValR 6:60), Vibhīṣaṇa and Hanumān, the only survivors, search through the bodies lying on the battlefield (6:61:7) and discover Jāmbavān in a partly conscious state (6:61:13-14). His first question to Vibhīṣaṇa is whether Hanumān is still alive (6:61:18). When the *rākṣasa* is perplexed as to why Jāmbavān should not ask about the Rāghavas, Sugrīva, or Aṅgada, instead of Āñjaneya (6:61:19-20), the bear expresses his conviction that if Hanumān lives, then though they all be dead, they are alive (6:61:22), for there is hope for survival (6:61:23). He then tells Māruti that the latter's power alone can save the monkeys as well as the Rāghavas (6:61:26-28), and for this purpose, dispatches him to get some herbs on a mountain peak in the Himalayas (6:61:29-34). Clearly, Hanumān would not be gaining such praise at the cost of a later Rāma, the leader of the army, on whom victory depends. Therefore, in the AdhyR, after the Rāghava has recovered from his voluntary submission to the *Brahmāstra* (6:5:58), He is the one Who orders Māruti to bring back the mountain peak of herbs (6:5:71-73), thereby keeping firm control of His army, possessing the necessary knowledge to rejuvenate it, and using Āñjaneya as an instrument for His will and purposes.

In Vālmīki's second scene, Hanumān is not given any eulogies, but is merely sent out by the physician Suṣeṇa (6:89:13-16).[3] Though Āñjaneya's superhuman status is growing parallel to Rāma's unfoldment as a symbol, his growth must nonetheless be subordinated to the latter's.

Tulasī's contraction of the two passages is particularly visible in the identity of the one who instructs Hanumān. Rather than choosing between Jāmbavān (ValR 6:61:26) and Suṣeṇa (ValR 6:89:13), both are used: when Jāmbavān asks who will fetch the physician Suṣeṇa (who, strangely enough, is no more in Rāma's army,[4] but a resident of Laṅkā), Māruti carries out the task, and he is then sent by Suṣeṇa to bring the herbs (6:55:4—6:do.55).

Vālmīki's Āñjaneya reaches his destination, but unable to locate the herbs, in the first case because they hide from him (6:61:58), and in the second because he does not recognize them (6:89:17), he uproots the mountain peak and carries it back to Laṅkā (6:61:61-66; 6:89:20-22). The army (6:61:67) and Lakṣmaṇa (6:89:24) are then revived, and in the earlier scene (6:61:68), he returns the peak to its place.

In the RCM, the episode is elaborated by the insertion of two counter-balancing obstructions on Hanumān's path: Kālanemi (6:56:1—6:58:3) on the way to the Himalayas, and Bharata (6:do.58—6:do.60b) on the way back to the battlefield. The first obstacle is to be found in the western and Bengali recensions of the ValR,[5] as well as in the AdhyR (6:6:35—6:7:33), while the second appears only in the Bengali recension of the ValR.[6]

In the Kālanemi incident, Rāvaṇa summons the demon to stop Āñjaneya (AdhyR 6:6:40-41; RCM 6:56:2), and though protesting and advising the king of the *rākṣasas* to do otherwise (AdhyR 6:6:42-63; RCM 6:56:2-4), Kālanemi finally decides that it is preferable to die at the hands of a *Rāmadūta* than Rāvaṇa (RCM 6:do.56).[7] He sets off and produces a lake, a temple, and a garden, and he himself takes the garb of an ascetic (RCM 6:57:1). In the AdhyR (6:7:7-8), Hanumān thinks he is either lost or deluded, for he does not remember the hermitage from his first expedition (AdhyR 6:5:73-74). Upon requesting permission to quench his thirst (AdhyR 6:7:14; RCM 6:57:4), he enters the lake, where an alligator, an *apsaras* under a curse, takes hold of his foot (AdhyR 6:7:21-22; RCM 6:do.57). When he kills it (AdhyR 6:7:23; RCM 6:do.57), the released *apsaras* informs him of the false ascetic's identity (AdhyR 6:7:26; RCM 6:58:1). Hanumān then slays Kālanemi (AdhyR 6:7:33; RCM 6:58:3), who, like Mārīca (RCM 3:27:7-8) and Rāvaṇa (RCM 6:103:2), dies remembering Rāma (RCM 6:58:3).

Just as in the ValR, Tulasī's Māruti finds the mountain, but not the herbs, and therefore uproots the mountain peak in order to bring it back to Laṅkā (6:58:4). On the way, however, Bharata obstructs him, believing him to be a *rākṣasa* (6:do.58). Struck by the Rāghava's arrow, Hanumān falls down unconscious, calling on Rāma: *sumirata rāma rāma raghunāyaka* (6:59:1). Amazed at the latter's invocation, Bharata rushes to his side and revives him (6:52:1-4)—though not of his own power, but in Rāma's Name (6:52:3-4). He then questions Āñjaneya as to the Lord, Lakṣmaṇa, and Sītā's welfare (6:60:1), and Hanumān quickly explains what all has taken place (6:60:1). Keenly aware of the urgency of the latter's mission, the Rāghava sends him off on his own arrow so that Āñjaneya may reach Lakṣmaṇa without further delay (6:60:3—6:do.60a).

When he finally arrives (RCM 6:do.61), unlike in the ValR, Rāma expresses His gratitude by embracing him (6:62:1). After Suṣeṇa has applied the remedy and Lakṣmaṇa has been revived (6:62:1), Hanumān takes the physician back to the city (6:62:2), but there is no mention, as in Vālmīki's second scene, of the return of the mountain peak.

In sum, the bringing of the medicinal herbs, or rather the mountain peak of medicinal herbs, is a clear illustration of the development of the Rāma figure—"the opening up of new levels of meaning of the symbol", to use Whaling's expression[8]— and the consequent reaction of other characters to it. Initially, Hanumān, whose status has already reached certain heights, is particularly well positioned; then, he and his powers are subordinated to the all-powerful Rāma; and finally,[9] Hanumān's capabilities are admirable only insofar as they are Rāma's capabilities manifested in and through him. With Māruti as His instrument, Raghupati blesses Kālanemi and Bharata by allowing the demon to die at His *dūta's* hand—thus by implication His own hand, for He is the *bala* behind Hanumān's hand—and by granting Bharata indirect contact with Him, for though Āñjaneya is the external form, Rāma is the Dweller therein.[10] Therefore, the shift is from Hanumān to Rāma-through-Hanumān.

REFERENCES

1. According to Jacobi (1893, pp.46-47), this is a later interpolation. Based on textual evidence, he explains that Garuḍa originally revived the army.
2. In the AdhyR (6:5:68), Rāma merely remains silent for a moment (*kṣaṇaṃ tūṣṇīm uvāsa*), presumably to show respect to the *Brahmāstra*, as interpreted by R.B.L. Baij Nath (*The Adhyātma Rāmāyaṇa* 1913), C. Pāṇḍeya (*Adhyātmarāmāyaṇa* 1984), and Swami Tapasyananda (*Adhyātma Rāmāyaṇa* 1985), for Rāma's total invulnerability accords with the general outlook of the text. Furthermore, since Lakṣmaṇa seems to have been unaffected by the missile (6:5:69), then clearly nothing could have happened to the elder Rāghava.
3. In the AdhyR (6:6:33), it is Rāma again Who sends Hanumān to get the herbs.
4. In the ValR, Suṣeṇa is Tārā's father (4:41:2) and the leader of the western expedition sent out in search of Sītā (4:41:4).
5. Vaudeville 1955, p. 251.
6. Ibid., p. 252.
7. Compare to Mārīca's situation in RCM 3:25:1—3:do.26.
8. Whaling 1980, p. 319.
9. As far as the present study extends.
10. Bharata himself expresses this conviction: *mile āju mohi rāma pirīte* (RCM 7:2:6).

18

FINAL REFLECTIONS

Based on the scene-by-scene analysis, several conclusions may be drawn concerning the development of the characterization of Hanumān. There is a clear change of position from the ideal *saciva* to the ideal *bhakta*, a substitution of human motives for spiritual ones, and a shift in emphasis from *dharma* to *bhakti*. This is not to say, however, that these are radically opposing views, but rather an unfoldment of what was potentially present in the ValR and brought to fulfilment in the RCM through the AdhyR.[1] Devotion does not deny or displace right conduct: on the one hand, it integrates it at a lower level,[2] and on the other, it elevates it by redefining it. While Vālmīki stresses *dharma* (the thesis), the AdhyR focuses on the world-transcending and therefore *dharma*-transcending *nirguṇa* Rāma[3] (the antithesis), which attitudes Tulasī Dāsa brings together in his convergence on *bhakti* (the synthesis).[4] The latter exemplifies right conduct through his characters' behaviour, as well as recognizes the *nirguṇa* aspect of the Divine, yet he emphasizes the highest *dharma* as *bhakti* to the *saguṇa* incarnation of Raghupati. This world's behavioural code *is* relevant, but it is measured by and derives its *raison d'être* from the *bhakta's* paramount duty of service to Rāma. The devotee inherits the *saciva's* shrewdness of perception, intelligence, psychological insight, caution, loyalty, and sense of responsibility, but these qualities are no longer self-cultivated over an extended period of time, for they are God-given in the form of spontaneous expressions of innate divinity. The thinking capacity, with its occasional spillover into *kapitva*, now surrenders itself at Rāma's feet in order to carry out His commands. The newly developed lack of self-consciousness changes a difficult task into joyful play, a serious responsibility into the performance of a wonderful role in Raghupati's *līlā*.

While Vālmīki's Hanumān is Sugrīva's *dūta*, and then both the monkey king's and Rāma's *dūta* (ValR 5:33:49), Tulasī's Māruti is only Raghupati's messenger, for which purpose he has taken birth. His capacity as envoy is gradually increased from an ordinary minister to one with supernatural powers—though still subject to his monkey nature—to one who, though externally a *vānara*, is internally free from all *kapitva* and filled with *bhaktatva* so that his *bala* is no longer his own, but Rāma's. In other words, as the Rāghava's status is magnified, Hanumān's equally growing stature recedes further and further into the background in terms of his own individuality, yet it is brought more and more to the forefront by virtue of his relationship of complete surrender to the Lord. Māruti is glorified only insofar as Rāma is glorified, yet his glory is such that in a sense it outshines Raghupati's, for the perfect recipient is higher than the Giver in that he furnishes a perfect vehicle for and manifestation of the Giver. Since, apart from the killing of Rāvaṇa, Hanumān single-handedly accomplishes all that is to be done (he brings about the alliance between the *vānaras* and the Rāghava, finds Sītā, takes note of the Laṅkā fortifications, weakens the *rākṣasa* forces, and brings Rāma's army back to life), Tulasī's Māruti may be viewed as the objectification of Raghupati's *śakti*. The analogy is particularly apt, given that he is Vāyusuta, for the Wind is also the internal air, a form of *prāṇa*, which, as the force of life or the "sum total of the energy displayed in the universe",[5] is *śakti*. Furthermore, since he is *Rudrāvatāra*, his service may be understood as the submission of the destructive aspect to the preservation aspect (Viṣṇu's *avatāra*) at the command of the creative aspect (Brahmā).

The varying depictions of Hanumān according to his gradually developing relationship to Rāma are summed up in a famous verse, generally ascribed to the *Mahānāṭaka*, which illustrates his transition from Vālmīki's ideal *saciva-dūta* to Tulasī's *Rāmabhakta* as Rāma Himself. Addressing the Rāghava, Māruti affirms:

> From the point of view of the body, I am your servant; from the point of view of the individual soul, I am a part of you;

from the point of view of the Self, I am you. This is my conviction.[6]

In conclusion it may be helpful to complete the survey of the development of Hanumān's characterization by bringing it up to the present. As Āñjaneya continues to portray the ideal *bhakta*, new episodes expressive of his devotion are added to the *Rāmakathā*, and some of the old ones are expanded. Already in Priyā Dāsa's commentary on the *Bhakta Mālā*, the scene wherein Vālmīki's Sītā gives Hanumān a necklace (6:116:68-72) now includes a reaction on the latter's part. He begins to crush each jewel, looking for *Rāmanāma* in it, and when he finds nothing, he throws the necklace away. Shocked, the others question his rude behaviour, in reply to which he explains his intention. Since no one believes that Raghupati and His Name are all-pervading, Hanumān tears open his chest to display *Rāmanāma* written on all his pores.[7]

Amongst the new episodes, there is, for instance, Āñjaneya's discovery, in a pillar, of the *Brahmāstra* which alone can kill Rāvaṇa.[8] Similarly, the Bengali *Rāmāyaṇas* depict Hanumān's search for an arrow by which the Ten-headed may be slain.[9] His tail takes on increasing importance because of the burning of Laṅkā, as well as its protective role in the Mahīrāvaṇa event: during the Laṅkā battle, Rāma and Lakṣmaṇa are taken to the nether world by demon Mahīrāvaṇa and rescued by Māruti, whose tail, in the process, is made into a fort to shield the Rāghavas.[10] Furthermore, in the interview with Rāvaṇa, each time the *rākṣasa* raises his throne, Āñjaneya lengthens his tail.[11] Some South Indian iconographic representations show Māruti seated on his tail, which is rolled up in a spiral.[12]

As Hanumān's position continues to increase, he seems to outrun Rāma in popularity. A widespread print in the Bhojpuri area shows dominant Āñjaneya carrying the Rāghavas on his shoulders.[13] He is found to be more and more independent, worshipped as a village deity, a protector against diseases, ghosts etc., a magician, a remover of obstacles—all of which harken back to his *yakṣa* origins. He also gains a five-headed (*pañcamukha*) form and a lesser known eleven-headed one.[14]

Over time, Hanumān acquires a following among various different groups, including Muslims,[15] Rajput and Maratha chiefs, reactionary groups,[16] militant ascetics,[17] wrestlers,[18] and the Rasik section of the Rāmānandi *sādhus.*[19] While to Muslims he is Mo-atbar Madadgaar ("reliable helper"), and to wrestlers, Bajaraṅgabalī ("mighty one of adamantine body"), to Rasiks, he is the intermediary between Sītā and the disciple.

As for Hanumān *avatāras*, tradition points to Murāri Gupta[20] and Rāma Dāsa,[21] both of whom are said to have grown tails. Concerning Nābhā Dāsa, a story recounts how Śiva threw down from the clouds a drop of Āñjaneya's sweat, which took the form of a man upon reaching the earth. The latter, therefore, was called "Nābhābhū-ja" ("born from a cloud"), which was then corrupted to "Nābhā-jū" or "Nābhā-jī".[22] A more recent example is Ramakrishna, who, at one time, so identified himself with Hanumān that he began to behave just like a monkey, consuming only fruits and roots, moving about in jumps, spending much of his time in trees, and even tying a cloth around his waist so that it would look like a tail. He later told his disciples that the lower end of his backbone temporarily lengthened by nearly one inch.[23]

Today, Hanumān is worshipped on Tuesdays and especially Saturdays.[24] He is revered as Saṅkaṭamocana ("liberator from troubles") and propitiated for all possible purposes, such as success in exams and undertakings,[25] as well as to obtain long life.[26] Varanasi's Saṅkaṭa Mocana Temple stands only next to the Kāśī Viśvanātha and the Annapūrṇā in importance,[27] while Ayodhyā's Hanumāngarhi is the city's most prominent temple and monastic institution housing five to six hundred resident fighting *sādhus.*[28]

Some modern films, as late as 1978, depict Hanumān striding out of his image to help those who invoke him, or possessing people.[29] With his popularity on the increase, he has become India's Superman with his own comic strip publication (*Mighty Hanumān*) and a huge *Hanoomate Club* for children.[30] Given this trend, it is likely that his seemingly all-pervading presence will continue to be felt and seen for a long time to come, and that the modes of his manifestations will keep on multiplying as quickly as the human imagination, propelled by inspiration, can produce them.

Hanumān, Māruti, Pavanakumāra, Vāyusuta, Āñjaneya, Kesarinandana, Mahāvīra, Bajaraṅgī, Saṅkaṭamocana... all these are Hanumān.

REFERENCES

1. Based on Whaling 1980, p. 14.
2. Ibid., pp. 260-61.
3. Strictly speaking, "*nirguṇa* Rāma" is a contradiction in terms, for Rāma is an incarnation and therefore, as such, *saguṇa*. However, if the term is understood to refer to that of which Rāma is an incarnation, thus using the effect to refer to the cause, just as smoke is spoken of as fire, then the contradiction disappears. The Sant tradition of Northern India, for instance, focuses on "Rām" in the purely *nirguṇa* aspect.
4. Based on Whaling 1980, p. 323.
5. From Swami Vivekananda's commentary on Patañjali's *Yoga Sūtras* (1:34) in Vivekananda 1907, p. 223.
6. Taken from *Universal Prayers* 1977, p. 237, no. 306. (I have been unable to locate an edition of the *Mahānāṭaka*.) My own translation. The Sanskrit is to be found on p.v of the present study.
7. Grierson 1910, pp. 271-72; Hein 1972, pp. 75,83-87.
8. *Complete Works of Goswami Tulsidas* 1978-80, vol.6, p. 249.
9. Sen 1920, p. 51.
10. Mani 1975, p. 308. Though this is quite an early episode, for it is referred to in the *Śiva Purāṇa* (3:20:34) and elaborated in the *Kamba Rāmāyaṇa*, it was not, for obvious reasons, incorporated by Tulasī Dāsa in his account of the *Rāmakathā*.
11. Walker 1968, vol.1, p. 425.
12. Jouveau-Dubreuil 1937, p. 82.
13. Wolcott 1978, p. 656. See also Aryan, plates 25 and 42 from Amritsar.
14. Aryan, p. 19, plates; Brockington 1984, p. 259; Ghurye 1962, p. 235; Liebert 1976, p. 100.
15. Aryan, p. 9 (see also plate 65); H.K. Sastri 1974, p. 65.
16. Aryan, p. 8.
17. Van der Veer 1988, pp. 23, 150.
18. Aryan, p. 8; Ghurye 1962, p. 236; Ghurye 1979, p. 161.
19. Van der Veer 1988, pp. 159,175.
20. Celebrated poet and Sanskrit scholar, contemporary of Caitanya (Sen 1920, p. 52).
21. Grierson 1909, p. 621. Mahipati's *Santavijaya* repeatedly stresses the oneness of Māruti and Rāma Dāsa (2:53,55-58; 3:52-55).

22. Grierson 1909, p. 620.
23. Saradananda 1952, pp. 182-83.
24. Eck 1983, p. 255; Ghurye 1979, p. 179.
25. Ghurye 1962, p. 237.
26. Martin 1913, p. 227.
27. Eck 1983, p. 264.
28. Van der Veer 1988, pp. 23,151.
29. Ghurye 1979, pp. 179-80.
30. Sandahl 1990, p. 59.

BIBLIOGRAPHY

SANSKRIT SOURCES: TEXTS AND TRANSLATIONS

THE VĀLMĪKI RĀMĀYAṆA

The Vālmīki Rāmāyaṇa : Critical Edition. (1960-75). 7 vols. Baroda: Oriental Institute. General editors: G.H. Bhatt and U.P. Shah.

The Rāmāyaṇa of Vālmīki. (1952-59). 3 vols. London : Shanti Sadan. English translation by H.P. Shastri.

The Rāmāyaṇa of Vālmīki: Bālakāṇḍa. (1984). Princeton: Princeton University Press. English translation by R.P. Goldman.

The Rāmāyaṇa of Vālmīki: Ayodhyākāṇḍa. (1986). Princeton: Princeton University Press. English translation by S.I. Pollock.

The Rāmāyaṇa of Vālmīki: Araṇyakāṇḍa. (1991). Princeton: Princeton University Press. English translation by S.I. Pollock.

The Kiṣkindhākāṇḍa of the Critical Edition of the Vālmīki Rāmāyaṇa. (1983). 2 vols. Toronto: University of Toronto Dissertation. English translation by R.J. Lefeber.

Sundara Kandam of Srimad Valmiki Ramayana. (1983). Madras: Sri Ramakrishna Math. Sanskrit text with English translation by Swami Tapasyananda.

OTHER SANSKRIT TEXTS

The Adhyātma Rāmāyaṇa. (1913). Reprint New York: AMS Press, 1974. English translation by R.B.L. Baij Nath.

Adhyātmarāmāyaṇa. (1984). Varanasi: Vārāṇaseya Saṃskṛta Saṃsthāna. Sanskrit text with Hindi translation by C. Pāṇḍeya.

Adhyātma Rāmāyaṇa. (1985). Madras: Sri Ramakrishna Math. Sanskrit text with English translation by Swami Tapasyananda.

Brahmapurāṇam. (1976). Prayag: Hindi Sāhitya Sammelan. Sanskrit text with Hindi translation by T. Jhā.

The Brahma Sūtra (of Bādarāyaṇa). (1960). London: George Allen and Unwin. English translation with notes by S. Radhakrishnan.

The Bṛhadāraṇyaka Upaniṣad. (1945). 3rd rev. ed. Madras: Sri Ramakrishna Math, 1979. Sanskrit text with English translation by Swami Jagadiswarananda.

Buddhist Mahāyāna Texts. (1894). *The Sacred Books of the East.* Vol. 49. Reprint New York: Dover Publications, 1969. English translation by E.B. Cowell.

Hindu Myths. (1975). New York: Penguin Books. English translation by W.D.O'Flaherty.

The Hymns of the Ṛgveda. (1889). Reprint Delhi: Motilal Banarsidass, 1973. English translation by R.T.H. Griffith.

Kāmasūtram (of Vatsyāyana). (1964). Varanasi: Chowkhamba Sanskrit Series Office. Edited with Hindi commentary by S.D. Śāstrī.

Laghu-Yoga-Vāsiṣṭha. (1896). Madras: Adyar Library and Research Center. 4th ed., 1980. English translation by K.N. Aiyer.

The Mahābhārata. (1973-78). 3 vols. Chicago: University of Chicago Press. English translation by J.A.B. van Buitenen.

The Maitrāyaṇīya Upaniṣad. (1962). The Hague: Mouton and Co., Publishers. Sanskrit text with English translation by J.A.B. van Buitenen.

Minor Works of Śrī Śaṅkarācārya. (1952). 2nd ed. Poona: Oriental Book Agency. Edited by H.R. Bhagavat. Poona Oriental Series, No. 8.

Nārada Bhakti Sūtra. (1982). Bombay: Central Chinmaya Mission Trust. Sanskrit text with English translation and commentary by Swami Chinmayananda.

Ṛgveda. (1963-65). 8 vols. Hoshiarpur: Vishveshvaranand Vedic Research Institute. Edited by V. Bāndhu.

The Rig Veda. (1981). New York: Penguin Books. English translation by W.D. O'Flaherty.

The Śiva-Purāṇa. (1970). *Ancient Indian Tradition and Mythology.* Vols. 1-4. Delhi: Motilal Banarsidass. English translation by a board of scholars.

Śrī Rāma Gītā. (1986). Los Altos, California: Chinmaya Publications West. Sanskrit text with English translation and commentary by Swami Chinmayananda. (Part of the *Uttarakāṇḍa* of the *Adhyātma Rāmāyaṇa.*)

Śrīmad Bhagavad Gītā Bhāṣya of Śrī Śaṅkarācārya. (1983). Madras: Sri Ramakrishna Math. Sanskrit text and commentary with English translation by A.G.K. Warrier.

Srimad Bhagavata. (1980-82). 4 vols. Madras: Sri Ramakrishna Math. Sanskrit text with English translation by Swami Tapasyananda. (*Bhāgavata Purāṇa*).

Universal Prayers. (1977). Madras: Sri Ramakrishna Math. Sanskrit passages with English translations by Swami Yatiswarananda.

The Upaniṣads. (1949-59). 4 vols. New York: Ramakrishna-Vivekananda Center. English translation by Swami Nikhilananda.

Viṣṇusahasranāma with Bhāṣya of Śrī Śaṃkarācārya. (1980). Madras: Adyar Library and Research Center. Sanskrit text and commentary with English translation by R.A. Sastry. (Part of the *Mahābhārata.*)

SOURCES IN OTHER INDIAN LANGUAGES: TEXTS AND TRANSLATIONS

THE RĀMACARITAMĀNASA OF TULASĪ DĀSA

Sri Ramacharitamanasa. (1949-51). Chandigarh: Geeta Press. Avadhi text with English translation.

Shri Ramacharitamanasa. (1989). Delhi: Motilal Banarsidass. Avadhi text with Hindi and English translation by R.C. Prasad.

The Holy Lake of the Acts of Rāma. (1952). London: Oxford University Press. English translation by W.D.P. Hill.

The Rāmāyaṇa of Tulasī Dāsa. (1978). 1st rev. ed. Delhi: Motilal Banarsidass. English translation by F.S. Growse.

OTHER WORKS OF TULASĪ DĀSA

Tulasī Granthāvalī. (1973). 3 vols. Varanasi: Nāgarīpracāriṇī Sabhā.

Complete Works of Goswami Tulsidas. (1978-80). 6 vols. Varanasi: Prachya Prakashan. English translation by S.P. Bahadur.

Kavitāvalī. (1964). London: George Allen and Unwin. English translation by F.R. Allchin.

The Petition to Rām. (1966). London: George Allen and Unwin. English translation by F.R. Allchin.

OTHER WORKS IN INDIAN LANGUAGES

Jñāneśvara. (1948). *Jñāneśvarī.* Reprint New York: State University of New York Press, 1987. English translation by V.G. Pradhan. Ed. H.M. Lambert.

Kabir. (1983). *The Bījak of Kabir.* San Francisco: North Point Press. English translation by L. Hess and S. Singh.

Mahipati. (1932). *Rāmdās: Translation of Mahipati's Santavijaya.* Poona: N.R. Godbole. English translation by J.E. Abbott.

———(1933). *Stories of Indian Saints: Bhaktavijaya.* Poona: Office of the Poet Saints of Maharashtra. English translation by J.E. Abbott and N.R. Godbole. On Tulasī Dāsa: pp. 31-56.

SECONDARY SOURCES

Agrawala, V.S. (1970). *Ancient Indian Folk Cults.* Varanasi: Prithivi Prakashan.

Aiyangar, K.V. (1942). "Govindarāja". ABORI 23, pp. 30-54.

Aiyar, V.V.S. (1951). *Kamba Rāmāyaṇa: A Study.* Reprint Bombay: Bharatiya Vidya Bhavan, 1970.

Allchin, F.R. (1966). "The Place of Tulsī Dās in North Indian Devotional Tradition". JRAS, pp. 123-40.

———(1976). "The Reconciliation of *Jñāna* and *Bhakti* in the *Rāmacaritamānasa*". *Religious Studies* 12, pp. 81-91.

Aryan, K.C. and S. Aryan. (n.d.). *Hanumān in Art and Mythology.* Delhi: Rekha Prakashan.

Babineau, E.J. (1979). *Love of God and Social Duty in the Rāmcaritmānas.* Delhi: Motilal Banarsidass.

Bakker, H. (1982). "The Rise of Ayodhyā as a Place of Pilgrimage". *Indo-Iranian Journal* 24:2, pp. 103-26.

Basham, A.L. (1954). *The Wonder That Was India.* 3rd rev. ed. London: Sidgwick and Jackson, 1967.

Bhattacharya, S. (1934). "The *Mahānāṭaka* Problem". *Indian Historical Quarterly* 10:3, pp. 493-508.

Bhandarkar, R.G. (1913). *Vaiṣṇavism, Śaivism and Minor Religious Systems.* Reprint Varanasi: Indological Book House, 1965.

Bhardwaj, R. (1979). *The Philosophy of Tulsidas.* New Delhi: Munshiram Manoharlal Publishers.

Böhtlingk, O. and R. Roth. (1855-75). *Sanskrit Wörterbuch.* 7 vols. St. Petersburg: Kaiserlichen Akademie der Wissenschaften.

Briggs, G.W. (1938). *Gorakhnāth and the Kānphata Yogīs.* Reprint Delhi: Motilal Banarsidass, 1975.

Brockington, J.L. (1976). "Religious Attitudes in Vālmīki's *Rāmāyaṇa*". JRAS, pp. 108-29.

——— (1984). *Righteous Rāma: The Evolution of an Epic.* New Delhi: Oxford University Press.

Buck, H.M. (1968). "Lord Rāma and the Faces of God in India".

Journal of the American Academy of Religion 36:3, pp. 229-41.

Bulcke, C. (1950). *Rāmakathā.* 3rd ed. Prayag: Hindī Pariṣad Prakāśan, 1971.

— — — (1959-60). "The Characterization of Hanumān". JOIB 9:4, pp. 393-402.

——— (1960). "*The Rāmāyaṇa*: Its History and Character". *Poona Orientalist* 25, pp. 36-60.

Campbell, J. (1949). *The Hero with a Thousand Faces.* Reprint Princeton: Princeton University Press/Bollingen Series XVII, 1973.

Chaturvedi, M. and B.N. Tiwari, eds. (1970). *A Practical Hindi-English Dictionary.* 2nd rev. ed. Delhi: National Publishing House, 1975.

Coomaraswamy, A.K. (1928-31). *Yakṣas.* Reprint New Delhi: Munshiram Manoharlal Publishers, 1971.

Daniélou, A. (1963). *Hindu Polytheism.* Reprint London: Routledge and Kegan Paul, 1964.

Dasgupta, S.N. and S.K. De, eds. (1962). *A History of Sanskrit Literature: Classical Period.* Calcutta: University of Calcutta.

De, S.K. (1931). "The Problem of the *Mahānāṭaka*". *Indian Historical Quarterly* 7.

——— (1937). "A Reference to the *Mahānāṭaka*". *Jhā Commemoration Volume : Essays on Oriental Subjects,* pp. 139-44. Poona: Oriental Book Agency.

Dimmitt, C. (1982). "Sītā: Mother Goddess and *Śakti*". *The Divine Consort: Rādhā and the Goddesses of India,* pp. 210-23. Berkeley: Graduate Theological Union. Edited by J.S. Hawley and D.M. Wulff.

Dowson, J. (1879). *A Classical Dictionary of Hindu Mythology and Religion, Geography, History and Literature.* Reprint New Delhi: Munshiram Manoharlal Publishers, 1973.

Dunnigan, A. (1987). "Monkeys". *The Encyclopedia of Religion,* vol. 10, pp. 65-66. New York: Macmillan Publishing Company. Edited by M. Eliade.

Eck, D. (1983). *Banaras: City of Light.* London: Routledge and Kegan Paul.

Garg, G.R. (1982). *An Encyclopedia of Indian Literature.* Delhi: Mittal Publishers.

Ghosh, J. (1963). *Epic Sources of Sanskrit Literature.* Calcutta: Sanskrit College.

Ghurye, G.S. (1962). *Gods and Men.* Bombay: Popular Book Depot.

——— (1979). *The Legacy of the Ramayana.* Bombay: Popular Prakashan.

Goldman, R.P. (1980). "*Rāmaḥ Sahalakṣmaṇaḥ*: Psychological and Literary Aspects of the Composite Hero of Vālmīki's *Rāmāyaṇa*". *Journal of Indian Philosophy* 8:2, pp. 149-89.

——— (1989). "Tracking the Elusive Ṛkṣa: The Tradition of Bears as Rāma's Allies in Various Versions of the *Rāmakathā*". JAOS 109:4, pp. 545-52.

——— and J.M. Masson. (1969). "Who Knows Rāvaṇa?—A Narrative Difficulty in the *Vālmīki Rāmāyaṇa*". ABORI 50, pp. 95-100.

Gorse, J.E. (1982). *Les Chants Nuptiaux de Tulsi-Das.* Paris: L'Asiathèque.

Gray, L.H., ed. (1917, 1928). *Mythology of All Races.* Vols 6 and 8. Reprint New York: Cooper Square Publications, 1964.

Grierson, G.A. (1893). "Notes on Tulsī-Dās". IA 22, pp. 89-98, 122-29, 197-206, 225-36, 253-74.

——— (1894). "Indian Epic Poetry". IA 23, pp. 52-56.

——— (1903). "Tulasī Dāsa, Poet and Religious Reformer". JAOS 24, pp. 447-66.

——— (1909). "Gleanings from the *Bhakta-Mala*". JRAS, pp. 607-64.

——— (1910). "Gleanings from the *Bhakta-Mala*". JRAS, pp. 87-109, 296-306.

——— (1912). " 'Il *Ramacaritamanasa* e il *Ramayana*' by L.P. Tessitori". JRAS, pp. 794-98.

——— (1913). "Is the Ramayana of Tulasi Dasa a Translation?" JAOS 33, pp. 133-41.

——— (1926-28). "On the *Adbhuta-Ramayana*". *Bulletin of the School of Oriental and African Studies* 4:1, pp. 11-27.

Handoo, C.K. (1964). *Tulasīdāsa.* Calcutta: Orient Longmans Ltd.

Hawley, J.S. (1988). *Songs of the Saints of India.* New York: Oxford University Press. On Tulasī Dāsa: pp. 143-61 (poems: pp. 162-73).

Hein, N. (1972). *The Miracle Plays of Mathurā.* New Haven: Yale University Press.

Hopkins, E.W. (1915). *Epic Mythology.* Strassburg: Verlag von Karl J. Trübner.

Iyengar, S.K.R., ed. (1983). *Asian Variations in Ramayana.* Madras: Sahitya Akademi.

Jacobi, H. (1893). *Das Rāmāyaṇa*. Reprint Darmstadt: Wissenschaftliche Buchgesellschaft, 1976.

Jouveau-Dubreuil, G. (1937). *Iconography of Southern India*. Paris: Librairie Orientaliste, Paul Geuthner.

Kane, P.V. (1946). *History of Dharmaśāstra*. Vol. 3. Poona: Bhandarkar Oriental Research Institute.

——— (1967). "The Two Epics". ABORI 47, pp. 11-58.

Katre, S.L. (1960-61). "*Jñānadīpikā* of Tulasīdāsa". *Munshi Indological Felicitation Volume*, vols. 20-21, pp. 403-11. Bombay: Bharatiya Vidya Bhavan.

Kellogg, S.H. (1875). *A Grammar of the Hindi Language*. 3rd ed. London: Routledge and Kegan Paul, 1938.

Klostermaier, K.K. (1984). *Mythologies and Philosophies of Salvation in the Theistic Traditions of India*. Waterloo, Ont. (Canada): Wilfrid Laurier University Press.

Krishnamachariar, M. (1937). *History of Classical Sanskrit Literature*. Reprint Delhi: Motilal Banarsidass, 1970.

Liebert, G. (1976). *Iconographic Dictionary of the Indian Religions*. Leiden, Netherlands: E.J. Brill.

Lüders, H. (1939). "Die *Vidyādharas* in der Buddhistischen Literatur und Kunst". *Zeitschrift der Deutschen Morgenländischen Gesellschaft* 93, pp. 89-104.

Mallmann, M.T.de. (1963). *Les Enseignements Iconographiques de l'Agni Purana*. Paris: Presses Universitaires de France.

Mani, V. (1975). *Purāṇic Encyclopedia*. Delhi: Motilal Banarsidass.

Martin, E.O. (1913). *The Gods of India*. Reprint Delhi: Indological Book House, 1972.

Masson, J.M. (1975). "Fratricide among the Monkeys: Psychoanalytical Observations on an Episode in the *Vālmīkirāmāyaṇam*". JAOS 95:4, pp. 672-78.

——— (1980). *The Oceanic Feeling. The Origins of Religious Sentiment in Ancient India*. Dordrecht, Holland: D. Reidel Publishing Company.

——— (1981). "Hanumān as an Imaginary Companion". JAOS 101:3, pp. 355-60.

McGregor, R.S. (1976). "Tulsīdās' *Srīkṛṣṇagītāvalī*". JAOS 96:4, pp. 520-27.

——— (1984). *Hindi Literature from Its Beginnings to the Nineteenth Century*. Wiesbaden: Otto Harrassowitz.

Misra, R.N. (1979). *Yakṣa Cult and Iconography*. New Delhi: Munshiram Manoharlal Publishers.

Monier-Williams, M. (1899). *A Sanskrit-English Dictionary*. Reprint Delhi: Motilal Banarsidass, 1986.

Nagendra., ed. (1977). *Tulasidasa: His Mind and Art*. New Delhi: National Publishing House.

Pandey, S.M. (1977). "Abduction of Sītā in the Rāmāyaṇa of Tulasīdāsa". OLP 8, pp. 263-88.

Pargiter, F.E. (1911). "Suggestions Regarding *Rig Veda* X, 86". JRAS, pp. 803-809.

——— (1913). "Vṛṣākapi and Hanumant". JRAS, pp. 396-400.

Pollet, G. (1974). "Early Evidence of Tulsīdās and His Epic". OLP 5, pp. 153-62.

Pollock, S.I. (1984)." The Divine King in the Indian Epic". JAOS 104:3, pp. 505-28.

Ramadas, G. (1925). "The Aboriginal Tribes in the *Ramayana*". *Man in India* 5, pp. 22-44.

Raghavan, V. (1941-42). "Uḍāli's Commentary on the *Rāmāyaṇa*. The Date and Identity of the Author and the Discovery of His Commentary". *Annals of Oriental Research* 6:2, pp. 1-8.

——— ed. (1980). *The Ramayana Tradition in Asia*. New Delhi: Sahitya Akademi.

Sandahl, S. (1990). "The *Ramayana* — Cultural Heritage as TV Soap". *Toronto South Asian Review* 8:2, pp. 57-64.

Sankalia, H.D. (1973). *Rāmāyaṇa: Myth or Reality* ? New Delhi: People's Publishing House.

——— (1982). *The Ramayana in Historical Perspective*. Delhi: Macmillan India Limited.

Saradananda, Swami. (1952). *Sri Ramakrishna the Great Master*. 2 vols. 6th rev. ed. Madras: Sri Ramakrishna Math, 1983. English translation by Swaṃi Jagadananda.

Sastri, G.S. (1943). *A Concise History of Classical Sanskrit Literature*. Reprint Delhi: Motilal Banarsidass, 1974.

Sastri, H.K. (1974). *South-Indian Images of Gods and Goddesses*. Delhi: Bhartiya Publishing House.

Sastri, P.P.S. (1942). "Commentators on the *Rāmāyaṇa* in the Fifteenth, Sixteenth and Seventeenth Centuries". ABORI 23, pp. 413-14.

Sastri, S.V.S. (1949). *Lectures on the Ramayana*. Reprint Madras: Madras Sanskrit Academy, 1977.

Schechner, R. and L. Hess. (1977). "The Ramlila of Ramnagar". *Drama Review* 21:3, pp. 51-82.

Sen, R.S.D. (1920). *The Bengali Ramayanas.* Calcutta: University of Calcutta.

Shah, U.P. (1958). "Vṛṣākapi in *Ṛg Veda*". JOIB 8:1, pp. 41-70.

Shastri, R.M. (1944). "The Authorship of the *Adhyātmarāmāyaṇa*". *The Journal of the Ganganatha Jha Research Institute* 1:2, pp. 215-39.

Sita Ram. (1914). "The Originality of the Ramayana of Tulasi Dasa". JAOS 34, pp. 416-21.

Söhnen, R. and P. Schreiner. (1989). *Brahmapurāṇa.* Wiesbaden: Otto Harrassowitz.

Sutherland, S.J. (1989). "Sītā and Draupadī: Agressive Behavior and Female Role Models in the Sanskrit Epics". JAOS 109:1, pp. 63-79.

Tessitori, L.P. (1911). "Il *Ramacharitamanasa* e il *Ramayana*". English translation: "The *Ramacharitamanasa* and the *Ramayana*". IA 41 (1912), pp. 273-86; IA 42 (1913), pp. 1-18.

Thapar, R. (1978). *Exile and the Kingdom.* Bangalore: The Mythic Society.

Thiel-Horstmann, M., ed. (1983). *Bhakti in Current Research, 1979-1982.* Berlin: Dietrich Reimer Verlag.

Tivari, H.G. (1954). *Tulasī-Śabdasāgara.* Allahabad: Hindustānī Academy.

Van der Veer, P. (1988). *Gods on Earth.* Atlantic Highlands, New Jersey: The Athlone Press.

Vaudeville, C. (1955). *Etude sur les Sources et la Composition du Rāmāyaṇa de Tulsī-Dās.* Paris : Librairie d' Amérique et d'Orient.

——— (1982). "Krishna Gopāla, Rādhā and the Great Goddess". *The Divine Consort: Rādhā and the Goddesses of India,* pp. 1-12. Berkeley: Graduate Theological Union. Edited by J.S. Hawley and D.M. Wulff.

Vivekananda, Swami. (1907). *The Complete Works of Swami Vivekananda.* Vol. 1. 13th ed. Calcutta: Advaita Ashrama, 1970.

Vyas, S.N. (1967). *India in the Rāmāyaṇa Age.* Delhi: Atma Ram and Sons.

Walker, B. (1968). *Hindu World: An Encyclopedic Survey of Hinduism.* 2 vols. London: George Allen and Unwin.

Weber, A. (1852). *Akademische Vorlesungen über Indische Literaturgeschichte.* English translation: *The History of Indian*

Literature. London, 1878. Reprint London: Kegan Paul, Trench, Trübner and Co., 1904.

——— (1870). *Über das Ramayana.* English translation: " 'On the Ramayana' by Albrecht Weber". IA 1, pp. 120-24, 172-82, 239-53.

Whaling, F. (1980). *The Rise of the Religious Significance of Rāma.* Delhi: Motilal Banarsidass.

Wilson, H.H. (1861-62). *Essays and Lectures on the Religions of the Hindus.* Vol. 1. *Religious Sects of the Hindus.* Reprint New Delhi: Asian Publication Services, 1976. Edited by R. Rost.

Winternitz, M. (1904-20). *Geschichte der Indischen Literatur.* 3 vols. English translation: *A History of Indian Literature.* 2 vols. Calcutta, 1927-33. Reprint Delhi: Munshiram Manoharlal Publishers, 1972.

Wolcott, L.T. (1978). "Hanumān: The Power-Dispensing Monkey in North Indian Folk Religion". *Journal of Asian Studies* 37:4, pp. 653-61.

Wurm, A. (1976). *Character Portrayals in the Rāmāyaṇa of Vālmīki.* Delhi : Ajanta Publications.

INDEX